Sunset Ideas for
Patios
& Decks

By the Editors of Sunset Books and Sunset Magazine

Lane Publishing Co. • Menlo Park, California

Make your patio your outdoor room . . .
where you can enjoy the best of indoor comforts
in an outdoor setting. Whether you're planning to
build or remodel a patio or deck, or simply look-
ing for ways to perk up the one you have, here
are dozens of imaginative and colorful ideas
to draw from. And to help you determine what
direction to go with your patio, we've included
a section on the ABCs of patio planning as well
as on the characteristics of structural materials
and the finishing touches that give a patio
personality.

   We are grateful to the many landscape architects, architects, and homeowners whose
ideas and experiences contributed to this book.
In particular, we wish to thank our checkers—
Eric Armstrong of Armstrong & Sharfman, Landscape Architects; and Russell A. Beatty of the
University of California, Berkeley.

Supervising Editor: Elizabeth Hogan

Research and Text: Barbara G. Gibson

Design: Steve Reinisch, Terrence Meagher

Artwork: Joe Van Severen, Bob Morgan

Cover: Sunny redwood deck is one step up from
an aggregate patio and a few steps down from a
shady spot beneath the trees. The wood screen
and high hedge help provide privacy; tubs of
bright marigolds add splashes of color. Design:
Roy Rydell. Photographed by Steve Marley.

Editor, Sunset Books: David E. Clark

Contents

Planning Your Patio

First steps toward a pleasing outdoor room

When you decide to add a patio to your home—or give your old patio a face lift—you cannot overestimate the value of planning. As an extension of your house, a patio can give you all the comforts of indoor living out-of-doors; as part of your garden, it can become a favorite entertaining and sitting area for at least part of the year. Given proper planning, a patio can also make interior rooms seem more spacious and provide a gracious architectural transition between house and garden.

Although the classic patio is the open inner court of a Spanish-style house, by common usage the word *patio* has come to refer to any outdoor sitting or entertaining area, be it a wood deck, brick terrace, lanai, detached garden room, atrium, or gazebo. Whichever kind of patio you choose for your situa-

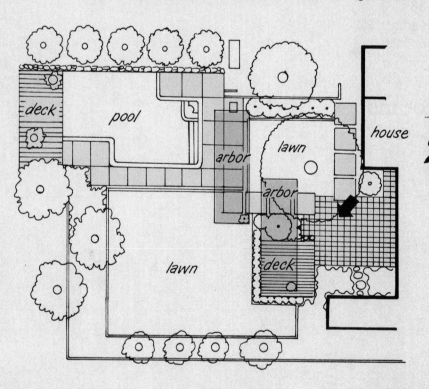

From plan (below) to patio (right)...*Careful planning paid off in this outdoor room—it offers both sheltered and sunny sitting spots, space for outdoor games, and an inviting garden atmosphere. Wisteria-laced arbor (right) shades a raised deck designed to extend an existing tile patio; another arbor lends shade by the swimming pool (see plan). Arrow on plan shows illustration's point of view. Design: Carl Rottschalk.*

deck

pool

arbor

lawn

arbor

lawn

deck

house

tion, allow yourself plenty of time to plan it carefully. Your patio is what you make it, and thoughtful planning will pay generous rewards, as well as protect you from costly mistakes.

The following pages present information you can use in planning: what makes a patio successful, how you can experiment without spending money, where to go for help when you need it, how to estimate costs (and how to trim them down), and what to expect from building codes.

Once you've read through this chapter and have a feeling for what you want in your patio, you'll be ready to draw on the hundreds of fresh design ideas that appear throughout the book.

The outdoor room

It used to be that patios—better known then as front porches or verandas—served as vantage points from which one could admire attractive gardens. Gardens, in turn, were often designed to be looked at rather than lived in; they were usually limited to front yards, where everyone could see them.

Back yards were either oversize play areas or service yards given over to garbage cans, clotheslines, and (during World War II) victory gardens.

Today, however, landscape design centers upon the need of homeowners for comfortable, inviting, and usable outdoor rooms that open to attractive gardens.

Although the challenge in creating a personal landscape is particularly great where rising property values limit lot sizes, careful planning and imagination can transform even a tiny subdivision lot into an inviting and distinctly personal outdoor room.

Successful patio design

Whatever the size of your lot, whatever your landscaping problem, good design will bring out the best in your patio: privacy, comfort, flexibility, safety, and beauty.

Privacy. As an extension of your indoor living space, your patio should give you a feeling of privacy just as interior rooms do,

but with no feeling of confinement. Even if your yard faces busy street traffic, you can make your streetside patio pleasantly private and still maintain a sense of spaciousness (see "Screens for shelter and privacy," page 26).

Comfort. You'll be more comfortable on a patio where adjustments have been made for particular climate problems. Getting and maintaining a comfortable patio "room temperature" often depends on using the right combination of design elements (location, overheads, vertical screens) to modify strong prevailing winds or excessive summer temperatures.

Flexibility. Good patio design should accommodate and adjust to your family's varying activities —casual gatherings, children's games, reading, outdoor dinners, barbecues, and so on. A good way to achieve flexibility is to give design elements multiple jobs: built-in benches that store sports equipment, fire pits that double as low tables. Creating access to your patio from more than one of your main indoor living areas also makes it more flexible.

Successful patio design

Whatever the size or shape of your outdoor living space, its design should ultimately offer you comfort, privacy, flexibility, safety, and beauty. Here, one plan illustrates how good design might be achieved in a street-facing patio.

Flexibility - patio adaptable to family dining, large-scale entertaining

Beauty - plantings provide color and texture; patio, house style harmonize

Comfort - right location (away from prevailing winds) helps create a pleasant patio climate

Safety - paving won't become slippery when wet

Privacy - garden wall screens patio from street

Safety. Make it a point to learn about the properties of various patio building materials—and avoid using any that might encourage accidents. For example, some paving materials become slippery when wet; others are too uneven for children's games, and some deck railings, though architecturally appealing, are not substantial enough to be safe.

Plan for safe traffic patterns between your house and patio and your patio and garden, and provide good lighting at steps and along garden paths.

Beauty. Most of the patios you see in the idea section (pages 34–79) are successful because they achieve a certain balance—both architecturally and esthetically—in the overall garden scheme. Materials used in patio construction blend with those used in the house, and colors and textures harmonize in the patio plants and decorative touches. Attention to construction and decorative details will contribute greatly to your patio's overall atmosphere.

Getting started

The first thing to do is decide what functions you want a patio to serve. Then you can examine your landscape to see what you have to work with and where you want your patio to go.

Evaluating your needs

Your first thought should focus on your family's needs and habits. Considering the way you live, make a list of what is most important to you (if you have children, get their input, too); then, if you need to compromise, you can compromise on the less important things. Here are some questions to consider.

Do you like to entertain with frequent outdoor dinners? Do the neighborhood kids like to play in your yard? Do you like to garden? How much time do you have to keep your patio in good condition? Do you prefer formal or casual living? Will your pets damage fragile patio plants or furniture? Your

answers to these questions will determine some basic design elements for your patio.

Sizing up the landscape

Next, take stock of your yard's assets and liabilities. Even if you plan to enlist the services of a landscape architect, architect, or landscape designer, you should have a good understanding of your existing landscape.

Can your patio plan capitalize on a fine view? Is your property bounded by woods? Perhaps your design can take advantage of a sunny southern exposure, a mature garden, or an impressive garden tree.

Consider also your yard's handicaps—is your lot on a steep slope? Is much of the lot exposed to street traffic? Is humidity a problem in summer? Does your present patio open off the wrong room, get too

much sun or shade, or lack sufficient space? You'll want to plan a patio that minimizes your special problems.

Choosing a patio location

Where your patio goes will depend largely on the size of your lot, the way your house sits on it, the uses you have in mind for the patio, and your climate. Even if you're stuck with a slab of concrete off the wrong room, you can still remedy a poor patio location.

Locations and lot sizes. If your house sits on a small lot, you probably have room for only one patio, most likely in a conventional spot off the living room, dining room, or kitchen. For an L or U-shaped house, however, a single patio can link and expand two or three interior rooms without consuming additional space (see illustrations below).

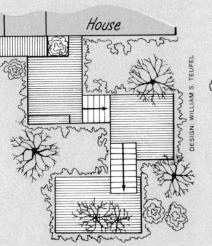

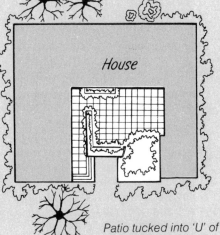

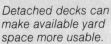

Detached decks can make available yard space more usable.

Patio tucked into 'U' of house links several interior rooms.

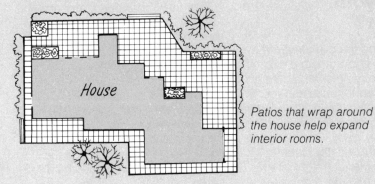

Patios that wrap around the house help expand interior rooms.

If most of your yard space is in the front, perhaps your patio belongs there, protected from street traffic and noise by a screen of shrubs or fencing. And don't overlook a narrow side yard or a garage roof—you may be surprised how a little imagination can transform dead space into a cozy outdoor room.

If your lot is steep with no ground room for a patio, plan a wood deck constructed above ground. It can relieve horizontal claustrophobia by extending one or more rooms or by wrapping around the house to open up the whole interior.

Homeowners with generous lots often find that several related patios suit their needs better than a single large one. If your lot is large, consider breaking up the space with two patios, one close to the house, the other at the far end of the garden. With patios at different spots in the yard, you can take advantage of their different exposures to sun and shade. Separate patios off the living room, kitchen, and master bedroom—planned for entertaining, informal outdoor dining, and solitude—provide alternatives for a family's changing and sometimes conflicting needs.

Remedies for hand-me-downs. If you've inherited a poorly planned patio along with your house, you can renovate it to suit your landscape plan. Try enlarging it, resurfacing it, or connecting it to a new patio by a garden path. If you're leaning heavily toward changing the patio completely, it's wise to remove the old patio and start with a totally new design.

How is your weather?

Understanding the climate around your home is important in patio planning. Two factors—the path of the sun over your house and the prevailing wind direction—govern the warmth or coolness of your outdoor room. If you know what to expect from the weather around you, you can plan a patio that will be enjoyable over a longer outdoor season.

The general forecast

If you've lived in your present climate through a number of seasons, you are already familiar with its benefits and hazards. But if you have moved to a new region recently, you may want to obtain accurate information to help you get acquainted with general weather patterns.

Excellent comprehensive climate information is available from the National Oceanic and Atmospheric Administration (NOAA, pronounced "Noah"), National Climatic Center, Asheville, North Carolina 28801. Send 20 cents with a request for the current annual issue of the Local Climatological Data naming your area.

You also can obtain accurate climate information from U.S. Weather Bureau offices, public power and utility companies, meteorology departments on college and university campuses, and country farm bureaus and agricultural extension offices. (Don't rely on the neighborhood "expert" or on rules of thumb or theories without scientific basis.)

Your relation to the sun

Theoretically, a patio that faces north is cold because it rarely receives the sun. A south-facing patio is usually warm because, from sunrise to sunset, the sun never leaves it. A patio on the east side is cool, receiving only morning sun; and a west-side patio is often unbearably hot because it receives the full force of the sun's midafternoon rays; in addition, late afternoon sun often creates a harsh glare.

Generally, your patio temperature will follow this north-south-east-west rule. Exceptions to it occur in climates where extreme summer or winter temperatures are predictable. For example, mid-July temperatures in Phoenix, Arizona, often climb above 100 degrees, and a north-facing patio there could hardly be considered "cold." In San Francisco, on the other hand, a south patio could hardly be considered warm, or a west patio hot, when a stiff ocean breeze has escorted a chilling fog to your patio party.

If you live in a temperate climate, a south or west-facing patio may be the best location, because the sun provides warmth during the afternoon and early evening when you are most likely to use your patio. If you live in a desert climate, a north-facing patio may be your best choice.

The sun by seasons. Another factor to consider in planning your patio is the sun's seasonal influence. As the sun passes over your house, it makes an arc that changes slightly every day, becoming higher in the summer, lower in the winter. Changes in the sun's path give us long days in summer and short ones in winter —and, as you can see from the illustrations below, they also alter sun and shade patterns on your patio.

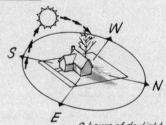

Winter

9 hours of daylight

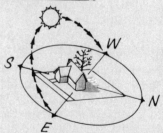

Fall and Spring

12 hours of daylight

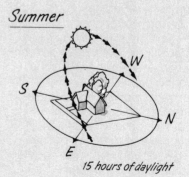

Summer

15 hours of daylight

Screening against wind

(Degrees are expressed in Fahrenheit)

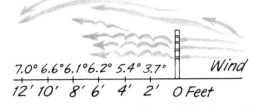

7.0° 6.6° 6.1° 6.2° 5.4° 3.7° Wind

12' 10' 8' 6' 4' 2' 0 Feet

For a fence with laths spaced about 1/2 inch apart, the lowest reading is close to the fence; the highest, 12 feet away. At 12 feet you would feel 7° warmer than when standing on the windward side of the fence.

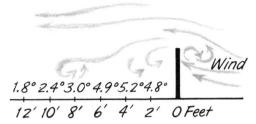

1.8° 2.4° 3.0° 4.9° 5.2° 4.8° Wind

12' 10' 8' 6' 4' 2' 0 Feet

Wind washes over a solid fence as a stream of water would wash over a solid barrier. At a distance about equal to fence height, protection drops rapidly. You feel only 1.8° warmer 12 feet away.

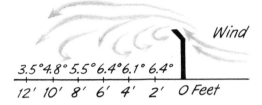

3.5° 4.8° 5.5° 6.4° 6.1° 6.4° Wind

12' 10' 8' 6' 4' 2' 0 Feet

A 45° baffle at the top of a fence eliminates the downward crash of wind. In this pocket, and 6 feet away from the fence, you feel 6.4° warmer than without a barrier. Beyond this point, temperature difference declines gradually.

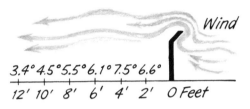

3.4° 4.5° 5.5° 6.1° 7.5° 6.6° Wind

12' 10' 8' 6' 4' 2' 0 Feet

Angling a baffle into the wind gives the greatest close-to-fence protection of any control tested. Beyond the maximum 7.5° increase, the comfort drop is gradual; effective protection extends to a distance more than twice fence height.

Understanding wind

Study the wind patterns around your house and over your lot. Too much wind blowing across your patio on a cool day can be just as unpleasant as no breeze at all on a hot summer day. Evaluating the wind will help you discover how to control or encourage it with fences, screens, or plants.

Three different kinds of winds may influence a patio location: annual prevailing winds, very localized seasonal breezes (daily, late afternoon, or summer), and occasional high-velocity winds, such as "Santa Ana" winds of Southern California.

Although you can determine the prevailing winds in your neighborhood by noticing the direction the trees lean, chances are that the prevailing winds around your house are different. Wind flows like water, spilling over obstacles, breaking into currents, eddying and twisting. After blowing through the trees, the wind may spill over the house and drop onto your patio.

You and the weather bureau. Probably no one experiences exactly the same temperature as the weather bureau. A reported temperature of 68°F. (20°C.) means that a thermometer in the shade, protected from the wind, reads 68°F. If there is a 10 to 15-mile-an-hour breeze, a person in the shade in the breeze will feel that the temperature is about 62°F. (17°C.). A person on a sunny patio sheltered from the breeze will feel a comfortable 75° to 78°F. (24-26°C.).

Screening against wind. Before you build a screen or fence to block wind from blowing across your patio, look at the wind control study above; it shows that solid barriers aren't necessarily the best ones. To determine what kind of screen or fence is best for your situation, pinpoint the wind currents in your yard. Post small flags where you want wind protection and note their movements during windy periods.

In the illustrations above, the lower line of figures indicates number of feet from fence; the upper line gives temperature differences between these points and the windward side of the fence.

Putting your plan on paper

After you've determined what you want in your patio, put your ideas down on paper. It doesn't cost much to experiment this way, and you'll find that the time you take mapping out your ideas will pay big dividends when your patio plan is finally executed.

Making a scale drawing

A good scale drawing will show you how well your patio design is working and how it fits into the whole house-garden relationship. When you fix the patio's location, the scale drawing will enable you to visualize logical traffic patterns; when you establish the size of the patio, you'll be able to keep it in scale with interior rooms and with

Making a scale drawing

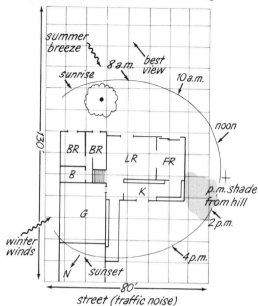

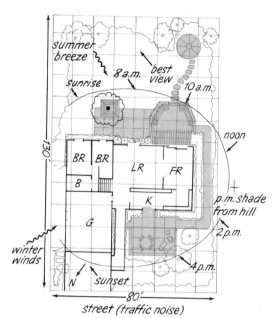

A good base map is the skeleton around which your patio plan develops. Use graph paper to show lot dimensions, house location, existing plants and trees, and any weather or privacy problems that might interfere with your out-of-doors enjoyment.

Sample patio plan, sketched on tracing paper placed over the base map, shows front and rear patios with a detached garden room. Tracing paper planning allows you to experiment freely with your ideas; mistakes on paper cost nothing.

the garden; and when you plan for exterior lights, you'll know where the wiring can and cannot go.

To make a scale drawing, you'll need graph paper (24 by 36 inches) and a pad of tracing paper. Use the graph paper to make a base map showing the physical properties of your lot and house. Use the tracing paper over the base to experiment freely with different designs.

Before you start your scale drawing, you'll save hours of complicated measuring if you can locate architect's drawings or house plans, deed and/or contour maps. *Architect's drawings* usually show site plan, floor plan, elevations, downspouts, and footing details. *Deed maps,* which show the actual dimensions and orientation of your property, are available through your city hall, county courthouse, title company, bank, or mortgage company. *Contour maps* show the shape of your site in 1-foot, 5-foot, or 10-foot contours—especially important information for hillside lots. You may be able to get a contour map of your neighborhood

from your county engineer or Department of Public Works.

The base map. Use the largest scale the graph paper will allow, usually ¼ inch per linear foot. Show the following on your base map:
• Dimensions of your lot.
• Location of house on lot. Show doors and windows and the rooms from which they open.
• Points of the compass—north, south, east, and west.
• Path and direction of the sun and any hot spots it may create.
• Utilities (water, gas, and sewers) and depth of each; underground wires; exterior outlets for water and electricity; meter boxes and air conditioning units you may want to screen.
• Setback boundaries. (Your city or county building department can tell you what they are.)
• Direction of prevailing winds.
• Existing plants and trees.
• Any problems beyond the lot line which may affect sun, view, or privacy, such as unsightly telephone wires, major plantings, or a neighbor's second-story window.

• If you live on a sloped lot, use a second map to show the shape of it—contours, high and low spots, natural drainage patterns.

Experimenting with your ideas.
With the bones of your landscape mapped out on the graph paper, place tracing paper over it and begin to try out your ideas. Keeping your priority list at hand, sketch as many patio designs as you can come up with. Remember, mistakes on paper cost nothing. When you do experiment:
• Plan generously—and then count costs. Creating a strong design will help you distinguish between the more and less important elements of your plan, making later adjustments easier. You may find, for example, that a masonry fire pit isn't as essential to your plan as an additional 5 feet of floor-level deck, or storage benches, or a wider garden path.
• Think in three dimensions. This will help you to balance the design elements and visualize the results. It will also keep you from confining your design to an endless horizon-

tal plane.
- Rely on familiar shapes. Landscape design based on squares, rectangles, triangles, circles, and hexagons almost always generate eye-pleasing designs that you won't tire of. Avoid squiggly or arbitrarily curved patterns.
- Stretch space. You can achieve the feeling of a bigger patio if your design leaves generous open spaces for planting, making the same amount of paving include a larger area.

For example, you can use 180 square feet of paving like this:

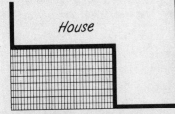

180 square feet of brick

Or, by adding 10 square feet of paving and two planting areas, you can double the size of your patio:

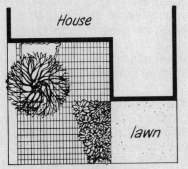

190 square feet of brick

Or, you can make the space seem larger by tying it to the lawn and to a unit of planting:

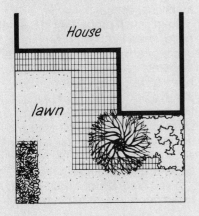

Or, you can enlarge the patio and still keep the feeling of brick by combining it with a less expensive material such as concrete:

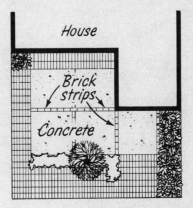

- Try to see your design as a whole. Since your patio is part of both the garden and the house, changes you make in it will have an impact on both. If, for instance, you plan a patio off the living room, shaded by a patio roof, will the roof make interior rooms darker? Will your patio eliminate your children's play space? If you consider your patio in relation to the rest of your property, you will find it easier to create a well-balanced plan.

Designing the modular way

Many people find it helpful to work with a single unit of space—such as a square or rectangle—repeated over and over again like squares on a checkerboard. Working with a uniform design unit helps you to be more exact in preliminary planning, and gives a sense of order to your design.

Modular planning is especially helpful if you are laying down patio paving for the first time. If you are using concrete, you can mix and pour it by the rectangle or square; if you are paving with bricks, you can lay one rectangle before starting another.

How to work with modules. In designing a patio with modules, you can use a design unit of almost any size or shape that suits your needs. Most professionals suggest a module no less than 3 by 3 feet; amateur landscapers think a more

generous module saves work.

To find out what size you should use, measure the length of the house wall that adjoins your proposed patio. If it is 24 feet long, six 4-foot rectangles will fit your wall dimension exactly. If you plan to work with brick, tile, or adobe blocks, make your module an exact multiple of their dimensions, including spacing if they are to be set in mortar.

Suppose, for example, that you decide to work with a 5-foot square. In the illustration below, you can see that your patio will divide into 5-foot squares; length of privacy screens will be a multiple of 5; walks will be 5 feet wide; planting beds will be 5 feet across; and tree wells will be either 5 by 5 or 5 by 10.

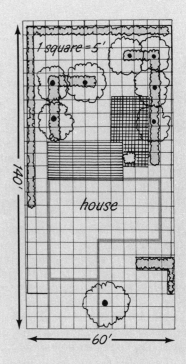

Slide projector planning

Along with map drawings, try using a slide projector to illustrate your ideas. Some architects and landscape architects use this technique to help clients visualize proposed designs or changes.

You'll need slides of the area you want to remodel, a projector, tracing paper, a soft pencil, and a fine or medium-point felt-tip pen. Set up the projector so it focuses

Guides to good design

As they survey yards and plan homesites, landscape architects tend to think in terms of four guiding principles: unity, balance, proportion, and variety. Understanding these principles can help you create an effective plan of your own. Design: Carl Rottschalk.

Unity – interconnected rectangles create pleasing, unified theme

Variety – different deck levels, construction materials, textures and shapes of plants arouse visual interest

Proportion – patio and decks are in proper scale to each other and to house

Balance – arrangement of decks, lawn, and pool is pleasantly unequal

on the wall at a level where you can work sitting down. Tape a sheet of tracing paper over the projected image and begin by sketching in just the proposed changes on the tissue. (With features such as doors, windows, roof, and ground lines already in the slide, it should be easy for you to maintain correct scale and dimension.) Whenever you decide your design isn't right, replace the tracing paper.

When you are satisfied with your new design, use a dark felt-tip pen to draw in the permanent existing background. Your eye will compensate for features that you just suggest with a few lines—your imagination sees an entire tree, even though you've only drawn in the trunk and a few branches.

Guides to good design

Four basic design principles— unity, variety, proportion and balance—guide many professional landscape architects and planners. If you follow these in your planning, you'll be well on your way toward achieving a design with flexibility and character.

Unity means that everything in your patio looks like it belongs together: paving, overhead, and screens complement each other; furniture suits the patio's architectural style; and patio plants relate both to each other and to plants in the garden. Unity between patio and house is important, too. If your patio is off a kitchen with a casual style, the patio should have the same feeling to it.

Variety keeps unity from becoming monotonous. Good design offers an element of surprise: a path that leads from the main terrace to one more intimate, a plant display that makes a garden work center part of the patio, a subtle wall fountain that gives dimension to a small space, trees that provide varying degrees of light and shade at different times of the day.

Variety also provides interest on a vertical plane. Patios at different levels, low walls, raised beds, privacy screens, and tubbed plants of varying heights help to draw the eye away from a horizontal expanse.

Proportion demands that your patio structure be in scale with your house and garden. Remember that your patio is an outdoor room, not an indoor one, and there will be a difference in scale. Al-

though many patios are scaled to the living room, don't be afraid to design a large patio. Outdoor furniture generally takes up more space than indoor furniture, and you may want room for containers of plants. Keep in mind, too, the range of activity that you want your patio to accommodate.

There are sensible limits, however. An oversized patio that looks more like a parking lot or playground can be grim. If your lot is so big that you need a large patio to keep everything in scale, try breaking up your space into areas that are more comfortable: squares of plantings inset in paving will break up a monotonous surface, and baffle plantings or fences can divide an area into two or more functional spaces.

To maintain proportion in a small patio, keep the design simple and uncluttered; clean lines will make elements seem larger. Stepped planting beds, for example, lead the eye upward and out of a confined area. Tall vertical screens used to enclose a small area will actually make it seem larger, as will solid paving, such as brick with its small-scale, repetitive patterns.

If you have a small patio, try to use moderate-size furniture (built-ins are especially effective) to avoid a crowded feeling. Use plants with restraint—overplanting will just add clutter. Remember to choose plants with their ultimate size and shape in mind. Poplar trees might suit the proportion of your patio when young, but they will grow far too tall for it within a few years.

Balance in patio planning comes when design elements are combined artfully to produce the same visual "weight" (not symmetry) on either side of a center of interest. If your patio is shaded on one side by a mature tree, you might balance the tree's "weight" with perimeter benches on the other side. If your patio is small and enclosed, but equipped at one end with a garden pool, you might balance the pool with patio furniture and accent plants.

Do-it-yourself design/construction

How much of the patio design and/or construction you can do yourself depends largely upon the time, energy, skill, and experience you can give to the project.

If you have a knack for design, there is no reason why you cannot develop a good patio plan, though it's a good idea to at least go for an hour's consultation with a professional landscape architect or architect. He or she can give you general parameters of good design and apply them to your situation, perhaps with a few rough sketches. If you are a skilled weekend carpenter, you should have no serious problems building a simple deck or patio overhead. If you aren't handy with a hammer, almost every remodeling project has a few easy, do-it-yourself opportunities. You can work on the parts of the job suited to your talents and temperament, leaving the difficult work to specialists.

If you decide to tackle the entire project—from design through construction—be sure you have the time and energy for it. Regulations governing building and remodeling can be exasperating—

and your design must accommodate those that affect your neighborhood (see page 15, "Building codes and zoning laws"). Learning new skills may seem intriguing until you run into complications that call for an expert's judgment. Estimating and buying the exact materials and tools you'll need can also be frustrating, especially when material prices change from week to week.

In other words, be realistic. Be honest with yourself about what you can and cannot do well, and operate within that framework.

Good sources of help when you design and/or build your own patio are:

• City or county building departments, for help in understanding local codes and zoning restrictions.

• Public libraries, for books and magazines on do-it-yourself building and remodeling.

• Garden and house tours, for design ideas. (Take your camera along to record ideas you want to remember.)

• Extension classes through community colleges or high schools, for evening courses in landscape design. (Local landscape architects often teach these classes; they can give you valuable advice for your particular project.)

• Other *Sunset* building books: *Basic Carpentry Illustrated; Ideas for Building Barbecues; How to Build Decks; Garden & Patio Building Book; Garden Pools, Fountains and Waterfalls; Landscaping; How to Build Patio Roofs;* and *How to Build Walks, Walls, & Patio Floors.*

Working with professionals

Most people who plan to add or remodel a patio seek some professional help, either at the design or construction stage of their project. Many homeowners rely on landscape architects, landscape designers, or architects to design the patio, draw up plans, and supervise construction. Others develop their own designs and hire a general contractor to see

that the work gets done. Still others (usually those experienced in home remodeling) act as their own contractor, ordering materials and hiring subcontractors with such special skills as drafting, carpentry, electrical work, tile setting, and plumbing.

Since trained professionals can develop good designs within the limits of a reasonable budget, it's usually more important to consult an expert if your pocketbook is small. Professionals know how to use different materials to best advantage, and they can help to avoid costly mistakes.

Landscape architects & designers

Landscape architects, architects, landscape designers, contractors, and drafters all may, in varying degrees, be able to give you professional design assistance.

Architects and landscape architects are state-licensed professionals with either masters' or bachelors' degrees in architecture or landscape architecture. Those who accept residential work may offer services ranging from short-term consultation to complete project supervision.

When retained on a planning-through-construction basis, an architect or landscape architect usually: 1) examines the site; 2) prepares preliminary and working drawings; 3) draws up bid specifications; 4) gets competitive bids and then arranges contracts with either a general contractor or subcontractors; 5) sees that correct grades of construction materials are ordered; 6) sees that construction work is done properly and on schedule; and 7) makes a final inspection of the completed work.

When retained on a consultation basis, an architect or landscape architect may help to polish rough plans, suggest ideas for a more effective design, or provide conceptual ideas and working drawings for the homeowner to carry out.

The fees charged by architects and landscape architects vary. Some charge a percentage of the cost of the work, some a flat fee, and others an hourly fee.

Landscape designers usually have a landscape architect's education and training but do not have a state license. Like landscape architects, they may develop designs and working drawings as well as supervise construction.

Landscape contractors—specialists in landscape construction—have design skills and experience too. Their fees are usually lower than a landscape architect's, but because their background is in construction, their design experience may be limited.

Draftsmen may be unlicensed apprentices to architects or members of a skilled trade who can make exact drawings of your plans. If you are an experienced builder and know the terms of the trade, you can save money by hiring a competent draftsman at an hourly rate to translate your design into drawings you or your contractor can work from.

Choosing a landscape architect. The best way to choose a landscape architect, architect, designer, or contractor is to see the person's work. If you aren't already familiar with someone you want to retain, check the Yellow Pages under "Landscape Architects," "Architects," "Landscape Contractors," or "Landscape Designers."

Although some excellent professional designers have no professional affiliation, many belong to the American Society of Landscape Architects (ASLA), American Institute of Landscape Architects (AILA), American Institute of Architects (AIA), or a state landscape contractors association. To locate members in your area, contact a nearby office.

General & landscape contractors

The role of the general or landscape contractor (specialists in garden construction) is to coordinate and supervise construction work.

If called to supervise a large project, the contractor assumes responsibility for hiring subcontractors (specialists in carpentry, electrical work, plumbing, and/or tile setting), ordering construction materials, and seeing that the job gets done. (A contractor who does a large volume of work may buy materials for you at low wholesale prices.)

For a less complex patio project, the contractor may bring his jack-of-all-trades experience to the job and do the work without subcontractors.

Choosing a contractor. If you have retained a landscape architect or architect, he or she can usually help you decide what kind of construction help you need and can recommend people who are conscientious and reliable.

If you haven't worked with an architect, finding a reliable licensed contractor may take some time. The better general contractors usually have commercial construction projects scheduled months in advance; they rarely take on small jobs.

Talk with homeowners who have had or are having work done, or material suppliers or subcontractors who depend on the business of contractors.

When selecting a contractor, base your decision on the individual's reputation in home building, not on the lowest bid. The contractor you choose should be well-established, cooperative, competent, financially solvent (check with his bank and finance companies), and insured for workman's compensation, property damage, and public liability.

Get preliminary cost estimates for your project from at least three contractors whose work you have found to be reliable. This involves no fee or obligation of any kind on your part and no firm commitment on theirs, and it will give you a good basis for further planning.

The contract. After you've made all final decisions, major and minor, get a firm bid from the contractor you prefer to work with. Then see that a complete legal, written contract is prepared. The contract should include dimensions, specifications, and type and quality of all materials, as well as a time schedule, cleanup agreement, bankruptcy release, and payment agreement. A contractor is usually paid either on the voucher system or in one lump sum on completion. After you've made a thorough inspection, you acknowledge completion of the job in writing.

Subcontractors

You may prefer to act as your own general contractor, hiring and supervising the skilled workmen for your project. If you plan to hire out the work this way, be sure you have the time and determination for it; if you don't, hire a licensed contractor.

Subcontractors can usually supply you with current product information, sell fixtures and supplies, and do work according to the specifications of technical drawings and the standards of local codes. Although their work may seem expensive to you, they have the training, experience, and specialized tools to do a faster and more professional job than you could do yourself.

When dealing with subcontractors, give them clear instructions, put all firm agreements in writing, and provide as much direct supervision as you can. Many subcontractors have a routine way of working which may not suit your objectives; you'll need to be clear and firm in your instructions to get the job done your way.

Trade associations can recommend licensed subcontractors in your area; check the Yellow Pages under "Associations" or "Labor Organizations" for the phone number of the local branch. Recommendations from other homeowners will also help you locate reliable and competent subcontractors.

Counting the costs

Once you've decided what you want and perhaps checked with an architect or contractor, try to establish a reasonable budget for your patio project. Remember that you don't have to do everything at once—it may be easier on your budget to execute your plan over two or three seasons.

How to figure expenses. First make a list of all the materials you'll need and estimate their cost. Include a list of alternatives, too—you may find that inflation has priced one item out of your range, that another has been discontinued, or that another isn't available for 6 months. Next, referring to your scale or preliminary drawings, calculate the exact quantities and sizes of each material you will need. You can get quick price estimates with a few telephone calls to building suppliers. (A single supplier may offer you a discount if you purchase all your materials there.) Make room in your estimate for sales taxes and changing prices—particularly if you plan to wait before purchasing materials.

Next, try to evaluate time and labor. This is probably the most difficult part of estimating, especially if you plan to do some of the work yourself. Generally, the cost of labor will range from 60 to 75 percent of the total cost of materials, but a reputable local contractor can give you a more precise estimate based on your materials list.

Money-saving tips. If you think your budget is too tight for your ideas, consider these financial shortcuts.

• Without overstepping the bounds of common sense, do as much of the planning as you can. You will save between 3 and 20 percent of your overall costs if you bypass a landscape architect or architect and develop your own design. You will also save on fees if, when you first consult a professional, you have your ideas carefully thought out (see page 9, "Putting your plan on paper").

• Doing the construction yourself may also save on overall costs. If you are an inexperienced home craftsperson, you still can save on labor charges by arranging with your contractor to perform some of the elementary tasks, such as painting, laying brick once the foundation is prepared, and digging trenches for underground plumbing or wiring.

• You can avoid additional costs by sticking to the working plans once construction begins. Changes you make in your design at this stage are usually expensive.

• Be sure that the contracts you sign are tight. You may save money in the long run by asking a lawyer to review the contract for loopholes, if you don't understand its terms clearly.

Building codes & zoning laws

Assigning your patio project to an architect or contractor who is familiar with local building codes and zoning ordinances is one way to reduce your worries about them. If you are planning to do the work yourself, visit your local building inspector or official as soon as your ideas are reasonably solid. He can help you with codes that apply to your specific plan.

Although you may consider any limitation a nuisance, building codes, zoning laws, and deed restrictions are designed to protect you from poor construction practices, property misuse, and deterioration of neighborhood standards. (Fortunately, there are legitimate ways to circumvent overprotective or outdated restrictions.)

Building codes. City and county building departments are charged with making sure that homes are structurally safe, free of health hazards, and within the legal rights of both homeowner and neighbors. Having reviewed thousands of home improvement plans over the years, building officials are well acquainted with complications you may encounter, and they can be of valuable service to you.

Even if you do engage a landscape architect or builder, it's a good idea to become familiar with your local building codes. The more legally accurate your rough plans are when you first visit an architect, the less your consultation fees will run.

In most areas of the U.S., the *Uniform Building Code (UBC)* sets the standard for home improvements. This "bible" of the construction trade is a formidable tome of regulations and engineering formulas that is brought up to date every 3 years. Your library should have a copy. If the UBC paralyzes you with its breadth and meticulousness, discuss your ideas with your building inspector. He can explain local ordinances that differ from the UBC.

Zoning ordinances. Zoning ordinances are designed mainly to keep commercial and residential properties separate, but in many jurisdictions these ordinances establish building setbacks from property lines as well as minimum height and lot coverage requirements that could affect your patio plan. Your building department (or, in some communities, planning commission) regulates these laws.

Deed restrictions. In some communities—particularly where a certain architectural character exists—you may find some restrictions in your deed that limit the kind or extent of improvements you can make on your property. You may be limited to working in a particular style (usually blending with the style of the house), or to using particular materials, or to building in specific locations on your lot.

Check your deed before you plan; its restrictions may override zoning laws.

Variances. If your proposed patio violates local zoning requirements, invades the required open space around the lot, or comes too close to the sidewalk, you can petition your local planning commission for approval of a variance. The building inspector may be able to help you prepare a variance, but your actual presentation is a matter between you and the commission. (You should have the approval of your neighbors; without it, your variance will probably be turned down.)

Building permits. Your patio project may not require a building permit; if it does, a single permit may cover the job as a whole. If the project is complex, however, you may need a separate permit for electrical wiring or plumbing. The fee for each permit is usually based on the value of the improvement.

Structural Elements & Finishing Touches

Your choices in paving, patio roofs, & decorative features

When you start planning your outdoor room from scratch, you will soon be face to face with the enormous variety of patio paving materials, overheads, privacy screens, climate modifiers, lighting fixtures, furnishings, and decorative accents that call for your consideration.

Some of these design elements will fall naturally into your patio plan; others won't fit at all. If you keep things simple and plan with your special tastes and needs in mind, you should be able to develop a workable scheme.

If you realize, too, that the way you combine the elements is just as important as the ones you choose, you'll have taken a big step toward creating an outdoor room with warmth, charm, and individual style.

Adding a split-level deck to a circa 1900 house gave owners new room for outdoor living and brought a fresh look to the house. Built of cedar, the deck was designed with perimeter benches, built-in garden lights, and an overhead trellis for a feeling of privacy. French doors lead from the dining area to the deck's upper level; its lower level, two steps down, overlooks a small city garden. Design: George Suyama.

Paving your outdoor floor

Brick, concrete, tile, flagstone, adobe blocks, and wood—all are excellent, durable patio surfacing materials if properly installed in the right place. When selecting the material for your patio floor, keep the following points in mind:

• Patio paving should have a pleasing surface texture, one that doesn't glare and is nonskid. A texture that appears soft will be more appealing than one with a hard, slick look.

• The color and texture of your patio surface should harmonize with the construction materials used in the house and garden structure (if you have one), as well as with the textures and tones in your garden plantings.

• Paving should be easy to keep clean—you shouldn't have to over-haul the patio every time food or mud stains need attention.

• Good paving should be weather-resistant so it won't sag, buckle, or crack in cold weather or absorb so much heat in warm weather that you can't walk on it. Consider, too, the foundation, drainage, and costs for a well-built patio.

• Give your patio floor a good foundation. The foundation almost always determines the appearance and life span of the finished job.

• To provide good surface drainage, slope your patio away from the house. Additional provisions, such as gravel pads and clay tiles (arranged underneath a patio to funnel water away from the house) may also be necessary to insure good drainage.

• Before you begin buying and building, count the costs—not only for materials and installation, but also for less obvious items such as a good drainage system and special construction. Added together, the costs should suit your budget.

• If you plan to do the work yourself, find a surfacing material that you can install with relative ease and without expensive specialized equipment.

Brick

Brick is probably the most adaptable and most frequently used patio surfacing material available. Set on sand or in mortar, brick provides a handsome, nonglare surface that blends with nearly any architectural style and looks at ease in almost any garden.

Though the basic form and composition of brick has remained unchanged for some 5,000 years, today's builder can choose from at least 10,000 combinations of colors, textures, and shapes to produce almost any mood—casual

Your choices in patio paving

You have many choices in patio paving materials, and limitless ways to combine them for imaginative effects. Here are seven of the most popular surfacing materials; each has its own assortment of sizes, shapes, and textures.

DESIGN: E. LESLIE KES

Impressed concrete

Flagstone

Aggregate

to theatrical—in a garden.

Of the two basic kinds of brick, common and face, common brick is most used by home craftsmen; it is also less expensive than face. The dimensions of common brick (generally 2¼ by 3¾ by 8 inches) vary among regions and manufacturers. The colors, traditionally red or reddish brown, now range from buff to bronze to gun-metal black.

A patio of brick on sand is one of the easiest paving projects for the beginner. And if the ground in your area doesn't freeze (or if excess ground moisture is no problem), bricks on sand provide as durable a surface as bricks set in mortar—and one that is as permanent as you want it to be. If you decide later that the patio needs a change, you need only destroy one brick to get the rest out in perfect condition.

You can lay bricks in stages, too, as your budget allows; and you can lay them in one of a half dozen basic bonds (patterns) or combine several to create innumerable variations (see illustration, page 20). Some of the more elaborate bonds, though, demand some fancy cutting and a good bit of accuracy.

In spite of all its glowing features, brick does have its disadvantages: costs per square foot run higher than most alternative materials, and, if you lay brick on sand, you will need to give periodic attention to weeds pushing through the joints. A brick surface can be uncomfortably uneven if haphazardly installed and can become slick with algaelike growth in moist, heavily shaded areas.

Concrete

Concrete paving offers permanence, long wear, and low cost, especially if you do it yourself. Putting down concrete is hard work, though, and if you have doubts about doing the job yourself, consider calling on a contractor.

Essentially a mixture of sand, cement, gravel, and water, concrete is even more variable in appearance than brick. It can be lightly smoothed or heavily brushed, washed to expose the aggregate, seeded with rock salt for a pocked effect, surfaced with handsome pebbles, swirled, scored, tinted, painted, patterned, or cast into molds to resemble other paving materials. And if you get tired of the concrete surface, it provides an excellent foundation for bricks or tile set in mortar.

You can buy the dry ingredients separately in bulk almost anywhere in the country. Concrete also comes in dry and wet ready-mix forms. These are more convenient, but also more expensive.

Two cautions: if not properly installed, particularly in hard-winter

DESIGN: TOM ORCHARD

Wood rounds

Adobe

Brick

Tile

areas, concrete will crack and buckle; and, once painted, concrete becomes slippery when wet and it needs a fresh coat every few years.

Patio or quarry tile

Tiles—kiln-fired ceramic squares—can give a patio either a smooth and elegant look or a rough and informal appearance. Either way, their warm, earthy tones blend well with garden colors. Tiles are easy to clean, they resist stains and scratches, and they withstand heavy foot traffic.

Outdoor tile usually belongs to one of two groups: quarry tile or patio tile. Both are manufactured products. Quarry tile is the more expensive to manufacture and is more regular in shape. Patio tile comes in more irregular, rough, handcrafted shapes reminiscent of

the primitive tile found in early California missions and Spanish haciendas. In addition to these, you'll find a variety of special-purpose and industrial tiles suitable for patio use.

For best results, tiles should be laid on a bed of mortar over firm, level ground or an existing concrete surface. However, you can also lay tile on a bed of sand or in mortar over a strong wood deck surface.

Flagstones

Slabs of stone—either limestone or sandstone, depending on locality—are the most expensive surfacing material you can buy, but they give unmatched permanence if properly laid. Their soft colors (buff, yellow, brownish red, gray) bring warmth to the patio, while their irregular shapes and sculptured surface add irregular pattern and texture to the garden floor.

Some people find, however, that flagstones look cold and quarry-like. The colors and irregularities may be difficult for anyone but a skilled mason to work into a pleasing pattern; badly laid stones can be an eyesore. As a compromise, concrete may be cast to simulate flagstone.

The irregular surface of flagstone makes outdoor furniture hard to balance, and it is not a good surface for games or wheeled playthings. Some types of stone absorb food, grease, or paint spills and are difficult to clean. (Discuss with your supplier the quality of the flagstone you are considering.)

If you choose to pave your patio with flagstones, have them installed by a skilled contractor. Proper matching, cutting, and aligning call for experienced hands.

Adobe blocks

With their warm and friendly air, adobe blocks look particularly appropriate in the patio of a ranch-style home. Easy to install, the blocks are laid in a bed of sand in much the same way as bricks. When spaced with 1-inch open joints, adobe provides an excellent base for a living floor of moss or

any other ground cover that grows to fill in the joints and soften the appearance of the surface.

Though adobe blocks now contain an asphaltic stabilizer to keep them from dissolving under winter rains and cracking under summer heat, they still tend to crumble at the edges and gradually wear away. Since the blocks store heat, their use is generally restricted to cooler patios.

Adobe is found almost exclusively in Arizona, New Mexico, and Southern California, but it can be used effectively almost anywhere in the country. Delivery charges outside the West, though, can make adobe an uneconomical paving choice.

Wood rounds, blocks, & ties

With its pleasing color and texture, wood paving brings something of the forest into a garden. Wood may be used as paving in several ways: round discs in random patterns can be embedded in sand over gravel; square blocks can be laid like bricks; or railroad ties can be combined with other paving materials or ground covers for a bold-looking, durable surface.

Rounds or blocks of redwood and cedar will eventually have to be replaced, because the end grain is constantly in contact with ground moisture that seeps up through the sand or rock bed. The open grain soaks up water, and the moist wood gradually rots away from bacterial growth or succumbs to insect infestations. Treating the wood with a preservative before installation helps.

Blocks and rounds are sensitive to weather, too. Best in shady spots, they can crack and warp in sunny locations, or freeze and split in heavy frosts.

Railroad ties, pretreated against rot and insect damage, will endure the elements for many years. If you're thinking of installing ties yourself, keep in mind that they are a husky material to handle. Standard ties measure 6 by 8 inches by 8 feet long and weigh anywhere from 100 to 140 pounds

Brick bonds

Running bond   Common bond

Jack-on-jack   Herringbone

Basket weave   Half basket weave

English bond   Flemish bond

each. (In some areas 2-foot 6-inch lengths are available.)

Wood decks

Wood used for decking is durable and resilient underfoot, and it does not store heat the way other surfacing materials can. In addition, its light weight (2 to 12 pounds per square foot) gives the novice do-it-yourselfer a convenient material to work with. And because it is available in a generous variety of species, grades, and manufactured forms—in some areas you can even buy pre-cut, pre-assembled wood decks—wood adapts easily to individual budgets and architectural styles.

The options are many on patterns (see illustration below) and finishes, too. Depending on the effect you desire, you can leave a deck alone, allowing it to weather naturally, or you can paint, stain, oil, or bleach it.

Wood decks do need periodic maintenance. You may need to remove mildew or fungus, rust stains from nails, and splinters, or to correct uneven weathering or spotty discoloration. Unlike other surfacing materials, wood is vulnerable to fire and termites.

If you have a hillside lot, check with your building department before you commit yourself to a high-level wood deck. Some communities require a report from a soils engineer that certifies the ground is geologically safe. And, in most communities, plans for a high-level deck must be approved by a structural engineer.

Loose aggregates

Several loose materials are well suited as a temporary surface or as a supplement to existing paving in a children's play area, service yard, path, or potting shed.

Wood chips, by-products of lumber mills, are springy, soft, generally inexpensive, and easy to apply. To work successfully as a patio surface, they should be confined within a grid with headers. Wood chips can make a good protective cushion under swings and slides in children's play yards.

Gravel, either smooth pebbles or crushed rock, provides an excellent, low-cost temporary surface that can later form the foundation for hard-surfaced paving. It also blends well with other materials, drains well, and makes a good base for steppingstones. As a patio flooring, gravel is best used in low-traffic areas, since it is easily scattered and difficult to walk on. It also tends to be pestered by weeds growing through it. (You can avoid

Nine ideas for deck designs

Decking patterns and shapes range from simple to complex. Select one that best suits your style.

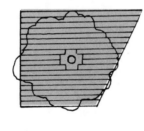
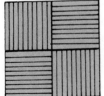

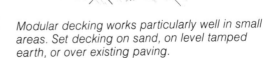

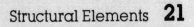
Modular decking works particularly well in small areas. Set decking on sand, on level tamped earth, or over existing paving.

the weed problem by laying gravel over a sheet of heavy plastic.) Gravel stands up best when it covers a more permanent bed of redrock or decomposed granite.

Redrock, available under a number of names depending on your location, is a rocky clay that compacts solidly when dampened and rolled. Along with decomposed granite (which is similar but longer lasting and more expensive), redrock can be put down alone or used as a foundation for another paving material. In time, the redrock surface will wear away and dissolve into dust.

Shade makers — patio overheads

Adding a simple roof to your patio can dramatically increase the number of weeks you can use your outdoor room. Properly planned and installed, a patio roof can give welcome shade to an expanse of hot paving, or protect a deck from frequent summer showers. But a carelessly planned overhead can turn a pleasant patio into a hotbox or a wind tunnel.

The sun's the limit

The way the sun shines on your patio or deck usually dictates the kind of overhead protection you need.

Generally, a *south-facing patio* requires a permanent overhead to give maximum protection from the sun. Because of its all-day exposure to the sun, a southern patio may be covered with a perishable material (such as canvas, reed, or bamboo) that will dry out quickly from heavy dew or rain. Lath running from east to west, or a solid covering of wood or fiberglass, will also provide effective protection.

A *west-oriented patio* receives the full force of the sun's midday rays and is likely to be scorching hot. Although an overhead will make the patio usable from 11 A.M. until about 4 P.M., you will need a vertical sun screen to block out the low, hot, late afternoon rays and their accompanying glare. If you live in a hot climate zone, design

the roof for good air circulation; avoid translucent covering materials that trap heat.

An *east-facing patio* benefits from morning sun but begins to cool in the afternoon. In many climates, overhead protection is not necessary but may be desirable for rain or fog protection or to hold the day's heat into the evening.

A *northern exposure* is the coolest patio site. Part of a north-facing patio will never receive any direct sun, even in midsummer. If the patio lies to the north of a two-story house, it may pass through all four seasons in complete shade. Such a patio does not need an overhead except to shed rain, block glare, or give a sense of shelter.

How to choose an overhead

Your patio roof can be permanent, adjustable, or portable; its material may be canvas, lath, eggcrate, translucent plastic, reed, bamboo, aluminum, or some combination of these.

Your first step in considering the various structures for sun control should be to consider the design of your patio, house, and garden. Your patio roof should harmonize with their colors and structural elements.

Once you've found several possibilities that suit your situation, consider the particulars: durability, maintenance, cost, and ease of installation. Consider your patio's future, too. Patios have a way of evolving into enclosed rooms, and you may want to construct a frame that will later serve as a bearing wall and support a more substantial roof. If so, hire an architect to avoid a tacked-on appearance that may even decrease the value of your house.

Fabric covers

Temporary but versatile, canvas can add cheerful color to an otherwise bland patio, lend shade where young trees will later cast shadows, and screen wind and rain.

Canvas, a tightly woven cotton fabric, comes in various weights and weaves in a vast assortment

Tempered glass

DESIGN: VING SMITH

Canvas

Patio roofs to filter the sun

The right roof over your patio will give you shade if you need it, or let the light through if you don't. Sometimes a roof is meant to do nothing more than give a feeling of protection. To get maximum overhead protection without blocking the light, consider a skylight-style roof of tempered glass panels in a wood frame.

DESIGN: ARMSTRONG & SHARFMAN

Louver

Lath

Bamboo

of solid colors, stripes, checks, plaids, and patterns. It can be made water-repellent and color-fast by coating with acrylics or vinyl; it can also be treated to resist fire and fungus.

Varying weights of canvas will provide light to dense shade over your patio, but the weight awning experts recommend is 10.10 army duck. Too heavy a canvas takes a long time to dry out after rain, and is thus likely to mildew. Too light a canvas, on the other hand, cannot withstand severe weather.

Although canvas is still considered the best fabric for most outdoor installations, some synthetic fabrics—acrylic fiber, woven fiberglass, and vinyl-coated nylon—also give pleasing results.

Shade cloth, used by nurseries for years, has become increasingly popular for residential use. The two kinds of shade cloth, saran (green) and polypropylene (black), are woven much like window screening. Various weaves give almost any degree of shade, from 6 percent to 94 percent.

Lath, batten, & lumber

Among the oldest and most versatile overhead covers is wood lath. Inexpensive, easy to install, and adaptable enough to give you as little or as much protection as any other cover, lath makes a good overhead where you need vertical air circulation and don't need a watertight cover. (Lath softened with deciduous vines is a popular combination for overheads as well as vertical screens.)

The term "lath" includes several varieties. The most common is rough-surfaced redwood, cedar, or cypress, milled to about ⅜ by 1⅝ inches and sold in lengths up to 8 feet. Batten is a sort of overgrown lath available in lengths up to 20 feet. Boards and framing lumber may also be used as lath. Lath overheads may also be constructed from rustic-looking grapestakes or from wood-and-wire utility fencing (sometimes called snow fencing).

Because of the unlimited number of ways that lath can be spaced, staggered, patterned, painted and stained, and because many sizes of these thin wooden strips can be used, your lath design may vary from a simple rustic trellis to an elaborate garden room. Some of the most impressive lath overheads are made of a single size of lath (1 by 1s, 1 by 2s, or 2 by 2s) with uniform spacing, but there is no reason why you cannot mix sizes and spacing.

If you choose a lath overhead, plan to use rot-resistant redwood, cedar, or cypress. These woods resist decay, require no painting, and are unlikely to warp or twist with changing weather.

A word of caution about a lath overhead—it casts sharply defined stripes of shadow. Some people find these shadows and the contrasty light annoying—especially when they are trying to read.

Louvers

If you want a permanent, airy, and tailored patio shelter that will block the sun at certain times and let it pour in at others, consider a louvered overhead.

Like a lath overhead, a louvered shelter is constructed of parallel boards. Louvered boards, though, are set on edge or at an angle to make the most of their width in blocking the sun.

Louvers may be adjustable or fixed. Adjustable louvers shift to give you almost any degree of light or shade you want through the day; fixed louvers can be designed to block sun when it's not wanted. But be careful when you plan a fixed louvered overhead—louvers are expensive and tricky to build, and once the boards are nailed down, they're not easy to change.

Eggcrates

An unfortunate name has become attached to these open-air overheads that, when laced with fragrant climbing vines, can add tremendous esthetic value to your patio.

Their very design makes eggcrate overheads natural showcases for dozens of vines that send out fragrant blossoms at various times of the year. Some deciduous vines leaf out for summer, yet let valuable winter sun through.

Standing alone, an eggcrate overhead allows free vertical air circulation and gives a protected feeling to a patio that needs all the sun it can get. An eggcrate shelter open to the sky may be the best solution for a patio on the north side of a house where the sun seldom shines, or for an eastern patio that gets only morning sun.

Eggcrates may be constructed of any common softwood, although the harder softwoods, such as redwood, cedar, or cypress are generally used because they need no protective coatings.

Translucent plastic

One of the quickest and most popular defenses against sun and rain on a patio is the translucent plastic overhead; it diffuses sunlight, intercepts heat, and keeps out rain.

Easy for the amateur to handle, plastic panels are lightweight, shatter-resistant, and quite durable. Often reinforced with fiberglass, they are available in a wide assortment of colors that transmit varying amounts of heat and light. (Take care, though, in selecting a color; translucent plastic panels cast their color onto the patio and perhaps—depending on window locations—into the house.) Plastic panels come both flat and corrugated, and in smooth and pebble-grained textures.

Since any solid roof attached to two or more walls of a house forms a potential heat trap, be sure to provide adequate ventilation if you plan to use translucent plastic. There is a greenhouse effect when plastic shelters plants; moisture is likely to condense on its lower surface and create an annoying drip.

Reed & bamboo

Among the lightest and most appealing overhead cover materials are reed and woven bamboo. Both materials are handsome, effective shade makers; in addi-

Vertical screens of plants & trees

Screens of plants and trees can cool your climate as effectively as they provide privacy and wind protection. Try running a deciduous vine like star jasmine (right) over steel straps; or plant Japanese maples in "bottomless" raised beds (below); or screen with tubbed bamboo (below right).

DESIGN: GUY S. GREENE

DESIGN: MICHAEL WHITMORE

tion, they're inexpensive and easy to handle. Many people prefer the soft, irregular shade patterns reed and bamboo provide to the harsher shadows cast by lath.

Woven reed and bamboo are among the easiest materials to install. They are sold in rolls that are simple to attach and are lightweight enough to require only a minimal understructure. These natural materials are not very durable, however, and cannot survive severe weather, such as hail or snow. Under normal conditions you can expect them to last for several seasons—bamboo longer than reed.

Bamboo comes in two grades: split and matchstick. The split grade is usually preferred because it is stiffer and coarser than the matchstick. For an adjustable overhead suspended from wires, use the more flexible matchstick.

Screens for shelter & privacy

Vertical screens—made of canvas, safety glass, bamboo or reed, wood, or plants and trees—can curtail intrusions onto your patio or deck by unwanted sun, wind,

or noise as well as by too-near neighbors. But to work effectively, screens must be planned and placed with care. Offhand planning may give you a screen that, far from solving problems, simply creates another discomfort in your outdoor room.

Another function of vertical screens is to define space: they can demarcate a front-yard patio, for example, or separate various areas of a garden (such as a busy play yard, a storage area, and vegetable patch). Screens can also camouflage unsightly objects such as air conditioners or swimming pool pumps.

Screens for shelter & privacy

Vertical screens can be helpful where you need privacy or wind protection. Adjustable glass panels (center left) swing on steel pins to let a little breeze by.

DESIGN: JOSEPH YAMADA

Aluminum screening

DESIGN: RAY COBB

Canvas

DESIGN: ALAN LIDDLE

Wood-framed glass panels

DESIGN: JOHN HERBST, JR.

Wood screen with trellis

DESIGN: HERB TURNER

Translucent plastic

Reed

Canvas, glass, bamboo & aluminum

Basically, what works for overheads (see pages 22–25) works for vertical screens. Glass or fiberglass panels, tie-back canvas, curtains, and roll-down shades of canvas, reed, bamboo, or basswood (a material similar to bamboo but giving a more polished appearance)—all can, to varying degrees, modify the climate on a patio that receives too much sun or wind. Translucent white fiberglass can be used to resemble shoji-style Japanese screens. Aluminum screening protects against the hot sun as well as against insects and windborne litter. Clear plastic or tempered glass panels are particularly effective where you wish to stop the wind but save the view.

Wood screens & fences

Free-standing wood screens and fences usually serve more substantial functions in a garden than do glass wind screens or roll-down shades. Vertical or latticed lath, louvers, and fencing sections punctuated with evergreen shrubs all give permanent but somewhat controlled privacy (as well as ventilation) to a garden that doesn't require complete protection.

Where seclusion is important, solid board fencing, grapestakes, translucent plastic panels framed with wood, or basket-weave fencing can give privacy to a streetside patio or screen a work area. Translucent plastic screens can admit light to a dark corner without allowing outsiders to see in.

Although few communities permit fences higher than 6 feet, you can apply for a variance if necessary to block the view from a neighbor's porch or second-story window. But first discuss your plans with your neighbor—tall fences are likely to generate ill will in the neighborhood. Remember too that tall fences are difficult to build.

Perhaps a more equitable solution to fence height problems lies with planted screens. A plant trained to rise above fencing re-strictions can be both legally and visually acceptable.

Lively screens with plants & trees

Plants and trees often make the best screens for patios and decks. They give a softer, more natural feeling to an outdoor room than do their manufactured counterparts. Though fences can seem blunt and imposing if you enjoy unobstructed vistas, screens of plants and trees are almost always pleasing features in a garden plan.

Vines trained onto lattice trellises or wire frames can make lovely vertical screens to block excessive wind or afternoon sun, while still giving an airy, open feeling to your patio. Many deciduous vines grow quickly to cover a large area (some grow too quickly) and leaf out in summer as your need for shade increases. In addition, some vines produce colorful and fragrant flowers, some produce fruit, and most require little care. Be careful not to use plants that attract bees or other insects; and remember that if you choose a rampant grower such as wisteria or clematis for your screen, you will have to prune frequently.

Evergreen shrubs make good screens where height is needed. Many shrubs reach treelike proportions and usually take a pleasing shape when left unpruned. Sheared evergreen hedges are generally used to give a patio a sense of enclosure. Higher hedges, especially dense ones, make excellent insulators against noise.

Trees, of course, are the most striking elements you can use to protect your outdoor space. The right trees in the right location will help break brisk winds, protect your patio from hot sun in the summer, and add sculptural value of its own. Unless your garden grows around a long-established tree, however, you will need to introduce a species of your own choosing. Select for growth rate, ultimate size, texture, color, shape, and habits (some trees are messy). Select carefully—once a tree is planted, it's usually there to stay.

The finishing touches

Once you've decided on the structural elements of your patio, you are free to turn to the finishing touches that reflect your more personal style and meet your day-to-day outdoor living needs. Most of these elements—such as the built-ins (furniture, barbecues, and storage), some exterior lighting fixtures, and garden pools—must be integrated into your basic plan.

Your decision can come later on your patio's more portable features—movable furniture, container plants, and other decorative accents.

Controlling your climate

A patio or deck that receives too much sun or wind can have its climate modified in many ways. Roofs and trees protect patios from the sun; screens protect against gusty winds. But you can also extend the usability of your outdoor room by adding some form of heating or cooling to take the edge off the temperature.

When you need heat. Firepits or fire rings, which often double as barbecues, are good sources of heat. If you want to be able to move the fire around, try one of the low, round metal braziers—or maybe two or more to help distribute the heat evenly. If your patio or deck can accommodate one, consider including a full-scale fireplace.

Portable pottery fireplaces from Mexico are relatively inexpensive and produce generous amounts of heat from only a small fire. But use them with caution: they're lightweight and reasonably fragile, and they may break if the fire inside is too hot. You get best results by burning kindling-size wood.

Don't forget that any open fire is a potential hazard. Be sure your fire is away from tree branches or patio overheads that could be ignited by flying sparks. Watch, too, for firebrands that may snap out onto decks and furniture; and on windy evenings, cover your fire with a fine wire mesh.

Gas-fed, butane, and electric infrared heaters, both portable and permanent, are another effective means of warming your patio. These heaters emit primarily infrared rays, reflecting them downward and out to warm you and objects around you, rather than the outside air. They work best in sheltered areas, since objects heated by infrared rays also warm the surrounding air a little.

Ideas for cooling. If soaring summertime temperatures keep you indoors more than out, you will benefit from a patio plan that incorporates one or several of these cooling methods:

Cool with water. Although garden pools, fountains, and waterfalls often appear in patio schemes for esthetic reasons, the water has extra value when it adds moisture to the air and helps cool a hot sum-

mer day. Even a simple garden sprinkler can cool your climate 10° to 20°, depending on the dryness of the air. Summer breezes blowing across garden pools absorb water and become cooler, as does the air around small spray fountains.

If you want to get water into the air without installing a garden pool, consider using misters (a type of spray head available at garden stores and nurseries) that throw a

The outdoor fire...
when you need heat

You'll spend more time on your patio if you have a way to warm it on cool evenings. Make room in your plans for a table-height firepit (below right) that can double as a barbecue, or a portable pottery fireplace (below) that you can install yourself, or a full-scale fireplace (right) that provides generous amounts of heat.

DESIGN: GALPEN, BALDON, & PRESBURGER

fine fog over moisture-loving plants. Often they can easily be attached to patio overheads or garden walls; they use a minimum of water (some only 3 gallons per hour), so they can be operated constantly without creating drainage problems.

Keep the air moving. Free circulation of air is another effective defense against summer heat, especially in hot, humid climates. If you are fortunate enough to have a prevailing summer breeze, plan your garden trees, shrubs, and fences so as to encourage it to pass through your patio. If your summer air is still, avoid creating a heat trap by keeping shelter structures open.

Cool with plants. Shading with shrubs, trees, and vines may be your best solution to summer heat. Exposed to the sun, plant foliage absorbs, reflects, and reradiates heat efficiently without overheating the area it protects. Plants raise the humidity of the surrounding air, but unless the air is near the saturation point the end result is a reduction in air temperature.

If you live in a mild-summer climate, the filtered shade you get from a birch, albizia, or olive may be enough. In hotter climates you may need the denser foliage of a fruitless mulberry or sycamore. Be sure, however, that the plants you choose to cool your patio climate are not so dense that they block essential air movement.

Fountains & patio pools

If cooling your patio climate isn't a problem, you still may want to include a garden pool or fountain in your patio plan for the esthetic qualities of its sight and sound.

Fountains. Water in motion is nearly always dramatic, and the simplest fountain can add a refreshing musical dimension to the smallest patio or deck. Moving water also provides a subtle but remarkably effective sound mask to traffic noises and close neighbors.

Garden fountains usually fall into one of three categories. *Spray fountains* are made versatile by assorted fountain heads that send water upward in shapes ranging

from massive columns to lacy mists. *Spill,* or *wall, fountains* send a single stream of water falling into a pool or series of tiered pans. *Splash fountains* force water up through a piece of sculpture; these are almost always professionally designed.

Garden pools. The size and shape of your garden pool is limited only by your imagination and your outdoor space. A still-water garden pool can be small and decorative or complex and "natural," depend-

ing on the effect you wish. (Keep the design simple, though, if you plan to do it yourself. Complex designs are not only difficult to manage during construction, but they rarely achieve the desired effect.)

If you want to start small, consider the tiny decorative garden pools that are available. They are both portable and versatile, and you can find them at garden supply shops and statuary stores. Or scavenge about your home for something you can convert to a small pool.

Two ways to cool your climate

Fine drizzle from tiny nozzles on overhead plastic pipe (right) waters moisture-loving plants at patio's edge and helps cool the surrounding air. Mist systems like this one apply water slowly with little runoff—an advantage in water-conscious, cost-conscious gardening.

Below, a forest of plants and a vine-covered trellis give leafy, heat-beating shade for a flagstone patio. Plant foliage absorbs heat and effectively reduces the air temperature.

DESIGN: C. JACQUES HAHN

Decorating with water: pools & fountains

Depending on the effect you want it to have, water can either accent an outdoor room or become its focal point. Recirculating water (below) spills over boulders into a "natural" pebble-lined pond. In another patio (right), water moves from one pool to another in a canal beneath stepping stones. The small spray fountain (bottom right) is simply a converted terra cotta tub.

DESIGN: ROLAND TERRY

DESIGN: WIMMER, YAMADA & ASSOCIATES

DESIGN: GENE HENNING

Traditional garden pools, made of brick, concrete, fitted stone, or tile, often blend as easily into contemporary patio settings as they do in formal surroundings. They also offer a fine opportunity to introduce new color and texture through the use of aquatic plants such as the hardy and tropical water lilies, floating hyacinth, and oxygenating plants and grasses. And a raised pool with brick walls provides a classic home for goldfish and koi.

"Natural" garden pools, streams, and waterfalls are the most enjoyable to create, but they demand the most sensitive design and maintenance, and usually a natural setting. It is no easy task to assemble rocks, soil, grasses, and other materials so that the pool or stream appears to be the work of nature.

Outdoor lighting

Good outdoor lighting is both functional and esthetic. It's functional because it will give you the right kind of light when you need it for entertaining, outdoor cooking, or a lively volleyball game. And it's esthetic because it will add to the beauty of your garden by highlighting architectural elements and garden plantings.

Thoughtful planning is the key to effective lighting. For help you might consult a landscape architect who has experience in exterior lighting. (Ask to see some of the archi-

tect's projects—at night—before you commission him or her to design an outdoor system for you.) Some electrical contractors and light fixture dealers also can offer valuable ideas; and your local electric utility often will give free design assistance on request. Your public library may also have helpful literature on the subject.

If you plan your own lighting system, here are some things to keep in mind:
• Decide first how much light you need. If you want to enjoy casual evening conversation, soft and indirect illumination will give you enough light to see without robbing the evening of its mood. If you're an outdoor chef, you will need a bright local light for the

barbecue area. And if you want an area lighted for outdoor games, you will need high-intensity illumination. (Avoid positioning lights that may shine in anyone's eyes.) To brighten hazard areas, such as dark pathways and garden steps, low profile lights are usually effective.

• Be strategic. A few lights judiciously located will create a far more pleasing atmosphere than a battery of fixtures indiscriminately installed to cast out the darkness.

• Include your garden in your lighting scheme. At night your patio or deck serves as a transition from the house to the garden, just as it does during the day—lights used to highlight trees or groups of plants will sustain visual dimension inherent in every daytime garden.

• Select lighting fixtures for style as well as function. You have many to choose from, ranging from utilitarian post lights, wall-mounted fixtures, and spotlights to ornamental accent lights made to look like everything from flowers to frogs to rocks. You will have an easier time with your choices if you keep the style of your outdoor room in mind. Some fixtures are designed to suit contemporary gardens, while others adapt best to formal plans. (When selecting lights to show off garden plantings, remember that the fixtures should be concealed. Only the results should show.)

• If you plan to do your own wiring (check with your building inspector to see if you need a building permit), you should probably stay with low voltage.

Low-voltage vs. 120-volt systems. Although more expensive than standard lighting fixtures, low-voltage systems (12 volts instead of 120), are generally considered safer for outdoor use. They're also easier to install, and they use less energy.

Standard 120-volt lighting systems are more durable and less expensive to purchase than low-voltage systems, but they are more difficult and expensive—and more dangerous—to install. Unless you are well acquainted with electrical wiring procedures, installation of

120-volt wiring is best left to a professional.

Light without wires. Warm, flickering light from open fires, candles, paper bag luminaries, or luau torches will add excitement to almost any night garden. Almost everyone responds emotionally to flame when it animates the atmosphere with dancing lights and shadows.

The biggest and most entrancing flame you can get is in the old-fashioned, campfire-style wood fire. Gas-fed fire pits provide both light and heat when volcanic rocks are piled into the shape of a pyramid. Funnel-shaped luau torches burn common kerosene, give a small darting flame, and make festive accent lights for parties. Decorating with candles can be lovely, too. Protect them with hurricane lamps or metal containers of your own making. Or try floating them in a garden pool or in glass bowls.

Storage

To keep equipment and supplies close to the spots you need them, you will want to include some kind of storage system in your overall plan.

Some of the best ideas are the simplest—such as patio benches that open up to store cushions or sports equipment, or cabinets attached to an existing wall to store barbecue paraphernalia. Or you can make use of space beneath a raised deck.

Many small-scale storage units are easy to build and portable. Larger units—which may be permanent or portable, freestanding or attached to an existing structure—appear unobtrusive when they double as screens to divide your patio from your garden work center. When designed to harmonize with your garden plan, they become part of your landscape.

Before you build a storage unit or position a prefabricated shelter, check local building codes and ordinances. Some specify exactly how close to a side or backyard fence these structures can be placed. In many locations you can put a shed anywhere you want as

long as it isn't anchored to the ground or to a concrete slab.

Furniture

When you select outdoor furniture, your first concern should be comfort—but keep an eye out for durability as well. Outdoor furniture can take a beating from the elements, and you will find that furniture designed and built to withstand weather, though often expensive, is more economical in the long run.

Most standard garden furniture is constructed of aluminum, wrought iron, steel, or wood. If you live in a damp climate, painted or enameled aluminum frame furniture might be a good choice because it will not rust. Rust may scar wrought-iron and steel furniture if the paint adheres poorly. Get specific information from your furniture dealer on rust-resistant coatings on any steel or wrought-iron furniture you are considering.

Although generally not as durable as standard furnishings, folding and collapsible garden furniture stacks for easy storage and can be useful when you need extra seating. Many people like wood-framed director's chairs with canvas seats and backs because they are comfortable, good-looking, colorful, and usually reasonably priced. Canvas will eventually deteriorate, but it is easily replaced.

In standard wood garden furniture, redwood is relatively inexpensive and popular in the West, scarce and costly in other areas. Often cumbersome and weighty, it belongs where it doesn't need to be moved frequently. It often splinters with age.

Combining built-in and movable furniture often solves a big problem for homeowners who want to use their outdoor rooms year round, but who must store garden chairs in winter. Built-in perimeter benches frequently find a place in patio and deck design because of their versatility: they serve as seating for sunny winter days (keep a supply of cushions handy to make them more comfortable), overflow seating when you entertain, buffet counters for outdoor suppers,

Storage: putting space to work

The outdoor answer to the indoor closet is a storage center—important if you want to have barbecue or play equipment handy, or if your needs include a garden work center. Box beneath a hinged bench (right) is perfect for children's toys; cabinets built into a brick barbecue unit (center) store picnic and cooking equipment. Space below a raised deck (bottom left) keeps small garden supplies; garden work center (bottom right), with storage drawers and display shelves, makes a handsome focal point in a small patio.

DESIGN: LAWRENCE R. MOSS

DESIGN: ARMSTRONG & SHARFMAN

DESIGN: ARMSTRONG & SHARFMAN

DESIGN: LANG & WOOD

platforms for container plants, and railings for decks. Because they also provide maximum seating in minimum space, built-in benches are excellent for small gardens.

Barbecues

When you choose a barbecue, consider your cooking needs, the size of your patio, your climate, and your checkbook. An outdoor cooking center can be anything from a hole in the ground to a masonry installation complete with a grill, spit attachment, oven, sink, storage unit, refrigerator, and, in some instances, a fireplace.

Unless your outdoor activities center around a large barbecue area, you will probably find a simple barbecue quite adequate for your needs. Regardless of its size and shape, a simple barbecue can perform the basic functions of outdoor cooking without straining your budget and without dominating other features of your garden. Barbecues range from classic masonry structures to manufactured metal units that may be permanent or portable.

If you want to build a stationary barbecue, plan its location carefully. Most barbecuing involves shuttling back and forth to the kitchen, so your barbecue should be handy to it. (An ideally located unit is both close to the kitchen and sheltered from the weather.)

One of the many excellent portables now on the market may be all you need. A portable barbecue makes a good choice if you prefer not to confine your outdoor cooking to one spot in your garden, if you don't want to rearrange your patio or deck plan to take in a permanent structure, or if you want to be able to move the barbecue under a shelter when the weather changes.

Whatever barbecue choice you make, remember to give yourself enough working space (built-in or collapsible) beside the grill for dishes, pots, and barbecue accessories.

Since most communities are very strict about what may or may not be done with outdoor fires, check with your local fire marshall and

Landscaping your patio

There are dozens of ways you can add interest to your patio when you landscape it with plants and trees. You might frame it with raised beds of bright annuals and accent it with shade trees (right). Or you can fill a planting pocket with Japanese maples and low-maintenance plants (below) to create a handsome patio focal point; raising a section of the overhead trellis gives maples room to grow.

DESIGN: HERR/SMITH ASSOCIATES

DESIGN: GENE HENNING

building inspector before you or your contractor begin work on a permanent barbecue unit.

Landscaping your patio

Within the larger framework of your landscape design, your patio makes a perfect stage to show off your favorite plants. Against a simple background, you can splash color onto your patio with pots of bright annuals. Or frame your patio with your favorite roses. If your ground space is limited, hang your plants overhead or make use of garden walls. To get shade where there is none, bring on a tree in a half barrel or tub. If you enjoy gardening, you can give your patio or deck a new look the year around by rotating container plants to display the best of each season. Be sure that the containers you use are in style with your patio and garden.

Patio plantings can also screen against too much wind or sun, disguise structural elements, and liven up drab corners or flat expanses of paving.

When you choose plants for your particular situation, be selective. To avoid the cluttered look of overplanting, use plants whose textures and foliage harmonize with each other and with your overall garden scheme. And choose plants that are well adapted to your climate.

Ideas for Outdoor Rooms

Great ways to take indoor living outside

Imagine having an outdoor living area that gives you many of the amenities of indoor living...
but in a garden setting. Where the walls are the restful green of trees and shrubs, the ceiling the sky, the decorative accents containers of colorful blooms that change with the seasons.

Whether you intend to completely remodel your garden or simply freshen up an existing patio or deck, you'll find on the following pages dozens of imaginative solutions to specific situations.

We've included ideas that apply to contemporary and traditional homes, spacious and small lots, level and hillside sites, formal and casual styles. Some of the patios cater to plant enthusiasts, others to low-maintenance gardeners. A few of the ideas are purely extravagant.

As you browse through the following examples of outdoor living areas, let the ideas inspire your thinking. Remember that the key to the success of these patios is that each is carefully thought out. All of the design elements combine to create a unified effect.

__Handsome terra cotta terrace,__ furnished for open-air dining and lounging, is a popular family gathering place. This outdoor living area speaks the language of texture...with earth-toned Mexican tile squares, a Brazilian pepper tree, border plantings of marguerite daisies, and bold white posts that divide outdoor spaces. Design: John E. MacAllister with Luis Villa and Lois Sherr.

Split-level entry courtyard doubles as outdoor living room for the owner of this contemporized Dutch colonial home. The upper deck (above), which leads to the entry hall and living room, has an open trellis overhead to give a feeling of protection. There's room for a hammock and garden furniture on the lower deck (left), which leads through a garden gate to the street. Decks, built-in benches, and trellis are stained to match house trim. Design: The Bumgardner Partnership, Rodney L. Juntunen.

Patios that open up indoor spaces

Contemporary or traditional, successful patio design relies on a good relationship between patio and house. Here two "indoor-outdoor" homes show how it's done.

In the home at right, architects capitalized on a spacious lot and favorable climate and designed patios and a deck that would open off almost every room in the house. Glass walls and sliding glass doors connect the outdoor and indoor rooms and give an expansive, airy feeling to the entire composition.

Below, a broad, shingle-skirted deck opens off the living room, where oversize windows admit a sweeping ocean view. In this way, the outdoors—easily visible from most interior rooms—becomes part of the indoor atmosphere.

Spacious redwood deck, *raised to room level to make the house-patio transition an easy one, is framed with perimeter benches that provide ample seating when a crowd gathers. From the deck, steps lead either down to a small sandy beach or up to a gallery deck off the second-story kitchen. Design: Royston, Hanamoto, Beck & Abey.*

Simple concrete squares arranged in an irregular pattern give a crisp, integrated feeling to this patio (below), shaded in part by the roof overhang and in part by a free-standing sunshade. You can reach the small floating deck (it's only about 8 feet wide) through the family room, from a path of concrete squares, or by way of stepping-stones that punctuate the garden pool. On the west side of the house (left), planting squares of African iris, gazania, and snap-dragons soften the bold design and add color and texture. Design: Wimmer, Yamada & Associates.

Slate and flagstone terrace, *perfectly situated where it can catch warm southern light, serves the dining room, library, indoor pool, and—by way of a pass-through counter at window level—the kitchen as well. Flagstone steps lead from the patio to a garden below. Curved redwood bench (right) provides seating around the fire pit and helps link materials used in the terrace with those in the house. Design: Laurence Underhill.*

Patios with easy access from house or garden

Ideally, your patio should be both part of your house and part of your garden, and for that reason it makes good sense to plan traffic patterns that move you easily from one to the other. The patios on these pages show how gracious these transitions can be. You can reach the slate and flagstone terrace from any of three interior rooms, or from the garden below by flagstone steps. The brick and concrete patio (below) opens easily off the kitchen and joins the garden with generously wide risers.

Broad steps, *decorated with containers of yellow marigolds and purple lobelia, make this patio-to-garden transition smooth and gracious. The brick and concrete patio opens off the kitchen, making open-air dining practically effortless. Sturdy, wisteria-laced trellis supports and shades an old-fashioned garden swing. A smaller tile patio off the living room (left) has a solid roof. Design: Eriksson, Peters & Thoms.*

Sunny, inviting brick-paved patio is partly shaded by a lath canopy keyed to the architectural style of the house. White slat benches, colorful cushions, and container plants all contribute to the patio's cheery, comfortable ambience. The transition between patio and garden (above) is smooth...when the brick patio wall ends, a wall of roses begins.

A perfect blend of function and charm

When the owners of this New England-style home wanted to extend their indoor living with an outdoor room, they asked landscape architects to design a patio that would give them a convenient outdoor cooking center, a shady spot for dining out, room to entertain, plenty of storage, and space for children's lawn games. Part of the appeal of the finished design is that it meets every one of these needs in only 425 square feet. Functional and charming, this outdoor room gives equal attention to both esthetics and practicality. Design: Armstrong & Sharfman.

Night lighting *from within and without lends special charm to this traditional setting. Because of good lighting, the patio is as livable after dark as it is during the day.*

Outdoor cooking center, *surfaced with red tile squares, is equipped with a built-in barbecue and plenty of storage space for cooking utensils and supplies. It makes a perfect buffet or snack counter for parties, and doubles as a garden center when container plants need attention.*

Generous concrete and brick welcome mat replaced a dull entry walk when the front yard was transformed into an appealingly private sitting spot. Cypress hedge screens the patio from the street. Design: W. David Poot.

Inviting entries... inviting patios

Most people plan patios for their back yards, to take advantage of space, privacy, and good indoor-outdoor traffic routes. But don't overlook potential in the front. Entry patios have a way of making guests feel particularly welcome, and they can turn unused yards into additional outdoor living space. If you haven't any back yard to develop, take heart—an entry patio may be the perfect solution.

Lofty arch spans house front and frames a shady entry alcove. It's an ideal entertaining area, easily reached from the dining room or from the kitchen around the corner. Small pool nearby is cool and musical. Design: Gene Henning.

Brick walkway connects garden entry with a delightful entry patio, made formal by wrought-iron garden furniture, a trim box-wood hedge, and occasional topiary plants. Bricks are laid in a basketweave pattern on sand and mortared at the edge. The garden sitting room (left) is also paved with brick. Its multi-paned door slides open and shut on an overhead track for easy climate control.

Handsome entry court, created with the addition of a brick garden wall and wrought-iron gate (above), gives owners of this Cape Cod-style cottage an outdoor room that's both private and spacious. Paving is brick-bordered concrete aggregate; plantings along garden wall include espalliered apricot, trimmed boxwood balls, rhododendrons, azaleas, and colorful summer annuals. Design: W. David Poot.

The private look of atriums & courtyards

Most classic of all patios is the atrium, or enclosed courtyard—a walled sanctuary where you can find protection from streetside views and noise, and privacy if it's situated away from the general flow of family traffic.

Interior atriums have been in use since ancient times. Framed by the four walls of a house, an atrium can be the private outdoor area in an urban setting; on a larger lot, it can provide an intimate garden counterpart to more spacious grounds outdoors.

Interior or exterior, one of the most important elements in the courtyard is its plantings. Here patio and garden share the same space, and you'll want to use plants to soften the harsh lines of paving and walls. Select them for adaptability to the special climate conditions a walled garden can generate, as well as for scale, shape, and texture. And try to avoid messy or sprawling varieties.

Expansive brick patio, *surrounded by house and garden walls, is softened with a profusion of containers and planting pockets filled with sweet alyssum and primrose. Canvas-cushioned furniture was chosen to suit this courtyard's generous size.*

Glass-walled atrium *exposes three interior rooms to a garden patio planted in shade-loving impatiens, woodwardia ferns, and a handsome copper beech tree. You reach the atrium through sliding doors off the living room or family room; kitchen window (above) opens to create a pass-through for food and beverages. Overhead, a skylight opens and shuts electrically for shade control. Design: Philip S. Grimes.*

Ideas for Outdoor Rooms **45**

Decks that wrap around the house

When the shape of your property or the style of your house calls for a wood deck, try stretching it. Decks designed to wrap around the house or its main living areas do much to open up interior rooms, extend living space, frame a pleasant view. If your lot is spacious, give yourself a generous wood terrace. If not, consider a smaller-scale version like the one shown on the opposite page (below); it's less than 8 feet wide, but it successfully extends living space the entire length of the house.

Plank deck, *designed to remedy a soggy and uneven lot, runs uninterrupted around three sides of the house Pale and vibrant pink rhododendrons border a portion of the deck, which is spacious enough to double as a children's playground. Design: William G. Teufel.*

Generous wrap-around deck adjoins three interior rooms and floats far enough above ground to take in a sweeping view of surrounding forests and a nearby lake. Framed at ground level with perimeter seating, the deck is constructed of 2 by 2 cedar boards stained to match the house siding. Design: William G. Teufel.

House-hugging cedar deck, designed after a Japanese engawa, makes a smooth, understated house-to-garden transition. Running the length of the house, the deck opens off an octagonal living room, the dining and family rooms, and the master bedroom. Brick path leads from the deck to a boat ramp. Bench railing (above) doubles as a table for casual picnics. Design: Howard A. Kinney.

Ideas for Outdoor Rooms **47**

Translucent skylight *lets the light in on this brick-paved patio, tucked between two bedrooms and open on one side to a balcony view of rugged canyons. A small metal fireplace warms up cool days or nights. Design: Gene Henning.*

Intimate adobe courtyard *opens off a bedroom to provide a private outdoor sitting spot away from family traffic. Focal point of this patio is the terra cotta fountain, converted from an oversize planting tub. Shade comes from the roof overhang and from grape vines that fill out during the summer. Design: Gene Henning.*

Leafy retreat off the bedroom is paved with irregular strips of exposed aggregate and oversize redwood headers. Garden bench fits neatly into a solid wood screen that separates this and a similar patio that adjoins the bathroom. Design: Thomas L. Berger.

Private patios off the bedroom or bath

If you're redoing your bedroom or bath, make the most of your remodeling by including a private patio off one or the other—or both. You'll find that a patio here can give you a get-away spot, perfect for quiet conversation, sunning, reading, or just reflecting. Fill the patio with plants and surround it with a wall, and you have a personal garden away from the din of family activity.

High-walled court, floored with wood and open to the sky, is accessible from both the master bedroom and bath. Wood beams overhead are designed to give this cozy sitting spot a feeling of protection. Azalea shrubs and standards add a flourish of color and break the height of the garden wall. Design: Peter Choate.

Broad, angular step links two wood decks, designed to level the uncomfortably sloping ground in this small back yard. Extending almost to the lot line, the deck is framed with perimeter benches and tall shrubs. Its fire ring is constructed of 12-inch-long firebricks, set on end and mortared. Design: Richard Carothers.

Low-level decks ...a solution to sloping lots

A favorite landscaping solution to damp or uneven back yards is the versatile wood deck. As a patio surfacing material, wood blends well with both formal and informal landscape plans; as a design element, it can give even the most irregular terrain a feeling of level spaciousness. If you live in an area where uneven ground is a problem, consider raising a deck over it. Though decking materials are usually more expensive than other kinds of paving, you will save on the high cost of having an area leveled or filled.

Poolside deck, situated in the sloping corner of a wedge-shaped lot, adds level space to this outdoor living area. Trellis overhead gives partial shade, and low-voltage lights—inconspicuously located in the trellis, wood screen, and deck steps—encourage frequent evenings out-of-doors. Design: Wimmer, Yamada, & Associates.

Low-level deck, *built of 2 by 2-inch cedar planks above soggy, uneven ground, weaves through wooded site. Deck accommodates long-established native trees and shrubs and—at one spot (left) —conforms to curves of a big boulder. A high horizontal lath screen provides privacy from neighbor's yard. Design: John Herbst, Jr.*

Prolific container garden gives a colorful introduction to the spectacular bay view this townhouse roof deck offers. Two-by-three fir planks, laid right over the old roof, were spaced to allow for good drainage. Over 100 terra cotta pots and two wooden crates contain mixtures of summer annuals, vegetables, and herbs. Design: R. David Adams.

View through the "window" of this boldly designed redwood deck is a landscape of gently rolling hills. The window's frame was created when architects extended the house roof line along the deck edge. Overhead, it's blue sky. Design: McKinlay, Winnaker, McNeil.

Outdoor rooms that capture a view

If your patio plan can take advantage of a view (the neighbor's trees may be all you need), give it high priority in your final scheme. An outdoor living area that draws your eye beyond its immediate floor plan allows you to observe and appreciate changes in your surroundings. And since a landscape is never static, the atmosphere in a view-oriented patio won't be, either. For ideas you can use, look at the imaginative ways homeowners here extended their visual lot lines.

Roof-level deck, *designed to capture a panoramic lake view, rises above treetops near this hillside home. Standing almost 20 feet off the ground, the deck is dramatically supported by a single, four-column pedestal. The deck's framework, flooring, and shingled railing are cedar. Design: Carlton C. Kovell.*

Pocket pool-side patio *capitalizes on a sweeping view of the rugged desert countryside. Low garden wall gives the patio a sense of enclosure and helps frame the view. Surrounding plants are native creosote and palo verde. Design: Michael Byrne, Robert Gladwin, and Carl Kominsky.*

Long-legged piers support and form part of the railing of this generous high-level deck, designed to float over a steep hillside. Two sets of sliding glass doors make the deck accessible from the living and family rooms. Roofed area (above) creates a pleasant shady nook. Design: Zaik, Miller & Butler.

Sun-catching cedar deck was built into a slope to create more level space in this narrow hillside lot. There's a smooth transition between slope and deck because of the deck's two levels –together they make an effective retaining wall, separately they provide seating, room for sunbathing, table space for picnics, and shelf space for container plants. Design: James H. Hensley, II.

Three ways to handle a hillside

Converting sharply sloping property into usable outdoor living space can be a challenge. If yours is a hillside lot, chances are the outdoor room designed for it will be either a cantilevered deck or a terrace carved out of the slope. Here, homeowners show how they made good use of their hillside sites—see how one took hold of the terrace idea and stretched it all the way down the hill.

Series of five platforms angles down the slope to give owners of this lakeside home easy access to the water. Broad concrete steps that connect the decks are lighted at night by low profile lights. Design: Zaik, Miller & Butler with Andrew Vincent.

Decks designed to go around trees

You're fortunate if you can build your outdoor living area around an established tree. A tree goes a long way in adding beauty, maturity, and character to a new garden plan—not to mention providing a natural umbrella for your terrace, a leafy screen to block unwanted views, interesting shadow patterns, and, as one drawing here shows, props for a swinging hammock.

The most important thing to remember when planning your patio around a tree is to be certain to give the root system breathing space. Paving over the roots may smother them and, therefore, kill the tree. One way to both preserve and emphasize a garden tree is to raise a platform around it, as in the illustration at left.

Benchlike platform makes this mature apricot tree a patio focal point. Here is a pleasant, shady sitting area, high enough off the ground to allow air to reach the tree's roots. Design: Jean Davidson.

Shade trees grow through the floor of a down-the-hill deck that floats just above ground in a natural forest setting. Steps lead up to a deck that's level with the living room. Design: William G. Teufel.

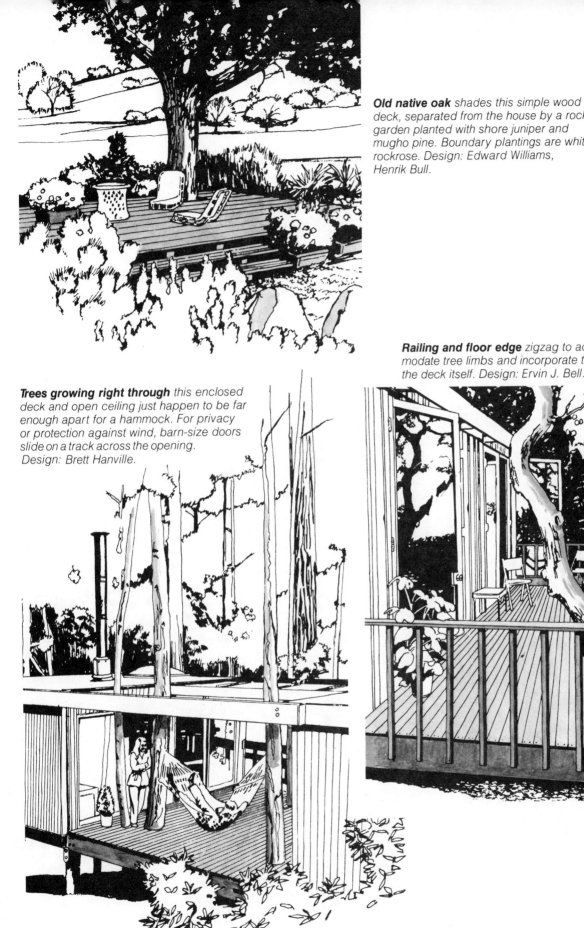

Old native oak shades this simple wood deck, separated from the house by a rock garden planted with shore juniper and mugho pine. Boundary plantings are white rockrose. Design: Edward Williams, Henrik Bull.

Railing and floor edge zigzag to accommodate tree limbs and incorporate them into the deck itself. Design: Ervin J. Bell.

Trees growing right through this enclosed deck and open ceiling just happen to be far enough apart for a hammock. For privacy or protection against wind, barn-size doors slide on a track across the opening. Design: Brett Hanville.

Big ideas for small spaces

Particularly in suburban areas, where undeveloped land at affordable prices is getting harder and harder to find, there's been a trend away from expansive lots toward smaller ones. But turning small yards into pleasant outdoor living areas can put landscape design skills to the test. Simplicity and detail are the keys to making maximum use of minimum space: simplicity because postage stamp spaces need clean, uncluttered lines to make them seem larger; and detail because in small places everything shows—workmanship, materials, and finishing touches.

Pads of pebble-seeded concrete lead to the main outdoor sitting spot in a condominium garden that can be reached from the living room, entry hall, or master bedroom. Colorful ground covers (creeping campanula, blue star creeper, and Korean grass) carpet unpaved areas. Design: Lang & Wood.

Charming, lattice-screened deck
replaced an unattractive service yard
that separated house and garage. The
new deck, raised three steps to room
level, snugs into less than 250 square
feet and still has room for a profusion
of flowering plants and ferns, as well
as an imaginative wall fountain (left)
designed with handpainted tiles. Trim
brick path (below) leads through
garden work center to street.
Design: Ron Yeo.

Pocket patios in the garden

If you've got the room, think about culti-
vating a pocket patio in your garden.
Patios detached from the house often put
more of your yard space to work and give
you a choice between sun and shade.
When it's within view of interior rooms, a
pocket patio makes a lovely garden focal
point; when it's not, you have a perfectly
private get-away spot. The five patios
here suggest the wide range of options
in design, materials, and location. Most
are small; the circular brick patio, for
example, is only 12 feet in diameter.

*Twin brick patios, one to stay
shaded and one to catch the
sun, give children a place to play
and adults a pleasant outdoor sitting area. Granite slabs in a carpet of Korean grass connect the
two. Design: Walter Reutimann.*

*Detached pocket deck, linked to
the main deck with a flagstone path,
makes a charming sitting spot in this
small garden. To give the outdoor
living area a unified look, wood
paving was stained to match the
house siding. Design: Mary Gordon.*

Shady enclave has a colorful stained-glass window–scavenged from an old schoolhouse–for a focal point. Arbor of Japanese wisteria, plus an ivy-covered wall, keeps the patio cool in hot weather. Design: Kathleen G. Garr.

Tiny redwood deck–it's only about 10 feet square–fits neatly into back yard niche, turning unused space into a sunny sitting spot. (See garden plan on page 12.) Design: Carl Rottschalk.

Private retreat is a circular pad of bricks shaded by eucalyptus and surrounded by tree ferns, agapanthus, clivia, and azaleas. Bricks are set on sand with a mortared edge. Recirculating water spills over rocks into a garden pool nearby. Design: George Fuller.

Ideas for Outdoor Rooms **61**

Enclosed entry court in this single family subdivision house makes a pleasant spot for close-to-home picnics. The small raised deck is large enough to accommodate both people and plants; around it, dichondra grows between paving squares. Design: Omi Lang Associates.

Condominium corner lot was transformed into a cozy outdoor room when a split-level redwood deck was added. A wood-framed glass screen, designed to block afternoon wind, keeps the interior view open and unobstructed. Benches that extend beyond the flooring to the lot line (above) maximize space. Design: Armstrong & Sharfman.

Patio ideas for cluster housing

How do you create inviting outdoor living areas when neighboring houses are only a few feet (or inches) away? The townhouse and condominium yard is characteristically small, and more and more often houses in planned developments are designed for diminutive lots.

As the trend toward cluster housing grows, so does the challenge to make small yards inviting and functional. Landscape architects who designed patios for the homes on these pages found—with water, glass, or simple materials repeated in a pattern—imaginative solutions to the closed-in feeling that small fenced spaces can give.

Townhouse garden, *once a 20 by 25-foot patch of bare dirt, is now a pleasant place for both people and plants. Water splashes down stone steps into a pool, then flows down a rock-lined stream that edges the deck. Overhead trellis shelters shade-loving ferns and ground covers. Design: Mary Gordon.*

Making the most of a narrow yard

If you're planning a patio for a long, narrow lot, knowing how to use the space is probably the most valuable skill you can have. To look their best, narrow yards often need to be made to seem shorter and wider than they really are...in other words, you can give your yard a more balanced look by breaking up its length and stretching its depth. Here are some practical ideas for outdoor living areas that fit neatly into squeeze-play spaces.

Low retaining wall *defines the patio these homeowners put down themselves after they carved a shelf out of the steep hill that was their back yard. To break up the yard's long look, the patio was designed with an L-shaped lath trellis overhead, an inset raised bed at one end, and a small koi pond at the other. Design: The Peridian Group.*

Boldly designed *garden bench became both focal point and privacy screen when this garden was remodeled to include a wood deck off the living room. Because it's near the lot line, the redwood bench makes the yard seem deeper. Design: Robert Perron.*

Used brick patio is one step down from a raised deck in this narrow but deep city lot. The change in levels, plus different surfacing materials and a profusion of container plants, helps divide the space. Design: Herbert Kosovitz.

Free-standing egg-crate overhead helps create a sense of spaciousness that otherwise might not be felt in a yard this narrow (it's only 18 feet wide). The pattern of the wood paving, the raised planting beds, and the angled wood bench at the far end of the deck add interest and variety to the overall scheme. Design: Herr/Smith Associates.

Ideas for Outdoor Rooms **65**

These roofs double as outdoor rooms

Sometimes it's possible to turn a roof into an outdoor living area. In these four cases, homeowners went up when they went out, either making use of existing but unused space, or carving out new outdoor rooms during remodeling projects.

The amount of weight your roof can support must be your first consideration when you focus on its potential as an outdoor room. You may need to buttress its substructure if the roof wasn't built to hold the combined weight of people, furniture, and a garden.

Landscaping your roof garden is often simply a matter of choosing the right container plants and trees for its climate. Choose plants that will withstand the eccentric conditions—strong winds, deep shade, or constant sun—found in rooftop situations. In addition, think of plants for their color, texture, ultimate size, and most of all for shape —trees with horizontal branching patterns, for example, will soften the vertical lines of a building, and columnar trees will offset a strong horizontal line.

Private pocket deck was created when homeowners made use of space in a steeply pitched garage roof. Cutting out a hole in the roof made room for the deck, which has a built-in storage cupboard, a hose bib for plant care, and a slightly sloped floor that drains to the outside wall. Design: John & Bonnie Glossinger.

Houseboat roof space was put to work when owners made it part of their extensive remodeling project. An exterior flight of stairs leads to the new deck, which was recessed into the roof and given a rubberized coating to make it weatherproof. Skylight cover doubles nicely as a built-in table. Design: Roger Patten with Robert Chittock and Bita du Flon.

Garage rooftop was transformed into a new outdoor living area when homeowners had it surfaced with preassembled decking. It took less than a day to put together sections of cedar 1 by 2s and garden benches (they're preassembled, too), and to bring on matching barrels of marguerites and marigolds. Iron railings were already there. Design: W. David Poot.

Ideas for Outdoor Rooms **67**

Approaching tradition with a contemporary touch, homeowners blended the best of both when they created an outdoor living area that centers around the swimming pool. Applying a little ingenuity (recycled French doors) to an old garage transformed it into a charming pool-side shelter and dining room that opens both to the pool and to the outdoor cooking center. The barbecue area has a built-in grill, storage space below the tile counter, and cushioned benches that follow the contour of the wall. Design: Bo Tegelvik.

Patios around the pool

A natural drawing card for sunning and entertaining, the pool-side patio also is an essential architectural element for the swimming pool setting. It provides a frame for the pool, a safe walkway for swimmers, and a necessary surface for drainage.

Here are some ideas that suggest the imaginative directions you can take with pool-side patios. When you plan yours, choose a surface that is not slippery when wet, and one that complements the feeling of your pool and garden. Provide a shaded area for protection from the sun. Try, too, to make the patio roomy enough to accommodate comfortably both sunbathers and furniture.

Generous redwood deck, *designed to fit a swimming pool installed in a narrow yard, provides plenty of room for sunbathers. Allowed to weather naturally, the deck was wedged into the hillside to give the yard a feeling of greater depth. Design: Wimmer, Yamada & Associates.*

Desert scenery *makes an appropriate backdrop for this dramatic swimming pool and patio, whose strong planes and huge boulders contrast with desert plantings. Where the patio changes levels, a concealed pump sends water spilling over boulders into the pool. Design: Guy S. Greene.*

Waterfront deck was added after these homeowners waited to see which areas of their yard they used most often. Arching around a slightly sloping lawn, the new deck has ample room for lounging and boat launching, and a springboard for diving enthusiasts. Design: Edward and Sue Rogers.

Cantilevered deck extends living space at this vacation home, situated on a lot too small to accommodate a patio. Framed with wide benches, the spacious platform is accessible from the main living area and from walkways on two sides of the house. Design: Howard Kinney.

Deck ideas for waterfront lots

If your property fronts a natural body of water, chances are you'll want an outdoor living area that capitalizes on it. Take your deck right down to the water's edge (or over the edge, like the one shown at left) and you'll be able to enjoy the benefits of a "borrowed" landscape...besides having quick access to water sports. Include a fire bowl in your plan and you'll have a perfect reason to stay outside during cooler days and evenings.

Octagonal deck was designed with a ring of bleacher seats to make room for family and friends when they gather around an early evening fire. At mealtime the top bench turns into a dinner table; adding a grate transforms the cauldron into a giant hibachi. Design: Mowry Baden.

Simple wood ledge makes the most of a natural stream that flows through this wooded back yard, creating a leafy retreat away from the house. Steps up from deck lead to terraces that adjoin interior rooms. Design: Thomas L. Berger.

Special effects with ornamental pools

When you're giving thought to your new outdoor room, consider the subtle effects you can create with water. Water has a marvelous, magical quality to it—incorporated into a patio scheme in even the smallest way, it can add generously to the atmosphere. Wall fountains, such as the one shown on page 59 (top photograph), take only a little space and give a small patio extra dimension. Freestanding fountains can range from a simple birdbath to a dramatic, avant-garde fountain sculpture. And small ponds with fish have a fascination all their own.

__Intimate walled court__ is only 24 by 31 feet, but it has ample room for people, furniture, container plants, and a 7-foot square pool with fountain. A swimming pool filter and pump outside the court keep the water sparkling clear. Design: Landscape Design Associates.

Gentle spray rises from a rotating fountain head at the end of a garden pool that's lined with hand-decorated Mexican tiles. Border bench provides pleasant sitting space. Design: Thomas Church.

Original ceramic sculpture was designed to send water spilling down its sides into a low pool. Recirculating pump forces water back up through ceramic columns.

Handsome island patio is surrounded by water—a swimming pool wraps around it at one end, a shallow reflecting pond at the other. Walls beneath the concrete steps keep the two pools separate.

Ideas for Outdoor Rooms **73**

The lanai idea

Look up the Hawaiian word *lanai* and you'll find it means a porch or veranda...or a roofed outdoor space used as a living room...or a living room that's open in part to the outdoors.

It's the room with the missing wall, and it's perfectly suited to climates with generous outdoor living seasons—in Hawaii the climate is mild enough to make lanai-sitting an all-year practice.

You may want to modify your lanai to suit your climate, perhaps with movable panels that will stop the wind and help reduce sun glare. With a series of sliding glass doors, you can even enclose your lanai and make it weatherproof. Where you want privacy or shade you can use translucent plastic panels or lattice screens.

Covered, furnished *outdoor space in a house of Spanish design is called a galeria or corredor...but by definition it's also a lanai. In areas where summers are hot, ceiling fans can help cool the lanai by moving the air. Design: Peter A. Lendrum.*

Cozy rooftop lanai opens from a bedroom to a view of the treetops. Canvas curtains on three sides are tied back in fair weather, zipped shut in foul weather. Adjoining roof deck (below) is open to the sun. Design: John E. MacAllister.

Honolulu lanai has 28 feet of sliding glass panels that disappear into the wall. Panels are pulled across the opening when rain threatens to blow in. Design: Vladimir N. Ossipoff.

Ideas for Outdoor Rooms **75**

The leafy look of garden patios

There's no reason why a patio and garden can't share the same space. In fact, a patio often makes an ideal setting for a plant enthusiast's container garden, or a stage around which to grow prize specimens. If you have a green thumb, look at the eye-appealing garden patios here for ideas you can use.

Enclosed entry patio gives gardening enthusiast room to cultivate an exotic subtropical garden planted with hibiscus, bougainvillea, passionvine, and creeping fig. Thoughtfully designed climate controls—removable translucent panels for the roof, sprinkler-misters, even a portable fireplace for winter use—maintain a comfortable patio temperature for both people and plants. There's room, too, for a sheltered aviary for parrots and doves at one end of the patio. Design: Gene Henning.

Small redwood deck with raised beds *gives suburban farmers plenty of room to produce crops of bush beans, cucumbers, and other vegetables. Arbor overhead shades the deck, and built-in bench minimizes the need for additional outdoor furniture. Design: Donald G. Boos.*

High-walled kitchen patio *seems big and airy (it's only about 12 feet square) because the natural lath canopy and hanging plants draw attention upward. On the floor, terra cotta tubs of maidenhair and sword fern balance and complement the overhead garden. Tile paving indoors and out artfully links the two rooms. Design: John E. MacAllister.*

Lath panels *—removable in winter to let in more light—and high walls give this leafy enclave plenty of privacy, plus protection for a shade-loving pygmy date palm, several kinds of ferns, a fancy-leafed begonia, baby tears, and coprosma.*

Ideas for Outdoor Rooms **77**

Four ways with gazebos

The gazebo has come a long way since its heyday as a romantic trysting spot for Victorian lovers. With the growing interest in outdoor rooms that can be enjoyed more fully, the gazebo has become a summerhouse where you can go to read or entertain or just get away from the activities around the house. It's instant shade for people and plants, a destination within your own garden.

Gazebos can be as elaborate or as simple as you like. Some have cooking facilities and sliding glass walls for weatherproofing; others are tiny structures made of leftover 2 by 4s and bundles of lath. Precut or prebuilt gazebos are also available; some manufacturers are quite small, with only local distribution, but you can probably locate one in your area.

Shingle-roofed gazebo *makes a handsome focal point for this hillside deck and an ideal "lookout" over the lake below. Deck railing complements the gazebo's traditional look; steps at right lead down the hill to a boat dock.*

Benderboards mesh around a circular opening at the top, making an airy crown for a gazebo equipped with built-in benches and an old-fashioned swing. Chevron pattern of 2 by 2s screens three sides; another side (not shown) has a tile-surfaced storage unit with electrical outlets for cooking appliances. Design: Alfie Krakow.

Classic lath gazebo is perfect for wine-tasting parties and garden weddings. Eight feet square, it stands on a slightly larger raised platform that makes it a good vantage point for watching lawn games. Design: Roy Rydell.

Octagonal summerhouse was raised in just three weekends by the home-owner and a carpenter. The pavilion, 12 feet in diameter, stands on a spacious raised deck and has a fence on three sides to create a sense of privacy. Design; R. W. Forsum Associates.

Index

Photographers

Glenn Christiansen: 52 top, 75 bottom left. **Jerry Fredrick:** 34, 37 bottom, 39, 40, 41, 43, 59, 60 top, 61 bottom left, 62 bottom, 69 top, 75 top, right, 77 left. **Barbara Gibson:** 37 top. **Dorothy Krell:** 67 bottom. **Steve Marley:** 48 right. **Ells Marugg:** 35 bottom, 36, 42, 44, 45 bottom, 48 left, 52 bottom, 60 bottom, 61 top, right, 69 bottom, 76, 77 top right. **Jack McDowell:** 38, 45 top, 47 bottom, 51, 53 right, 54, 62 top, 67 top, 68, 70 top, 78. **Don Normark:** 35 top, 46, 47 top, 70 bottom. **Norman A. Plate:** 53 bottom, 77 bottom.